A STUDY OF CASTE

A STUDY OF CASTE

P. LAKSHMI NARASU

AUTHOR OF "THE ESSENCE OF BUDDHISM"

GYAN

Published by

GYAN

Gyan Publishing House
5, Ansari Road
Daryaganj, New Delhi-110002
Phone: 011-47034999, 9811692060
E-mail: books@gyanbooks.com

Distribution Network
gyanbooks.com
India, USA, Canada, UK, Australia, France

ISBN : 978-81-212-4077-2 (PB)
First Published, 1922

2nd Impression 2020

Printed at: Gyan Press, Delhi.

A Study of Caste
Author: P. Lakshmi Narasu

To

SIR PITTI THYAGAROYA

as

an expression

of

friendship and gratitude.

FOREWORD.

This book is based on articles originally contributed to a weekly of Madras devoted to social reform. At the time of their appearance a wish was expressed that they might be given a more permanent form by elaboration into a book. In fulfilment of this wish I have revised those articles and enlarged them with much additional matter. The book makes no pretentions either to erudition or to originality. Though I have not given references, I have laid under contribution much of the literature bearing on the subject of caste. The book is addressed not to savants, but solely to such men of common sense as have been drawn to consider the question of caste. He who fights social intolerance, slavery and injustice need offer neither substitute nor constructive theory. Caste is a crippling disease. The physician's duty is to guard against disease or destroy it. Yet no one considers the work of the physician as negative. The attainment of liberty and justice has always been a negative process. Without rebelling against social institutions and destroying custom there can never be the free exercise of liberty and justice. A physician can, however, be of no use where there is no vitality. Similarly argument, philosophy, ethics, religion, legislation will not avail to transform a people who have not developed the will to live. Truth and freedom are the motive forces for the highest development of moral health, and on truth, virtue and knowledge depend all progress. Politicians, swayed by exaggerated creature comforts, fight for wealth, power and success, but give no thought to the psychological revolution so necessary for the progress of India. I have taken my stand on truth, unbound by convention and untrammelled by anxiety. I have nowhere attempted to tickle vanity or excite sentiment, nor have I resorted to compromise and equivocation. I have everywhere stated plain facts in a plain manner, but I mean no affront to any body. It is not my desire to force progress on those who are unwilling to bear it, but I hope to render aid to those whom experience has taught the necessity of forging a new life. The desire is abroad that India should become self-governing and a real political name instead of being a mere-geographical expression. If India is to evolve out of itself a democratic form of government, a government of the people by the people for the people, a political consciousness must be roused by a struggle to raise all towards the highest degree of possible culture. In all should spring up a sense of shame for every form of slavery, whether political or spiritual. Caste organization crushes the individual under its dead weight and hinders progress by killing all consciousness of liberty. Should my book serve to convince a few of its readers of the impossibility of creating a new people, united and cultured, without the abolition of caste and the uprootal of all religion whose life-blood is caste, it will have attained its end. I shall close with expressing my thanks to all who have rendered help in the preparation and publication of this book.

367, Mint Street, Madras. P. L. NARASU.

2nd January, 1922.

CONTENTS.

PAGE SUBJECT

1. Is caste universal ? Main features of caste. Hereditary specialization.
2. Hierarchical organization. Mutual repulsion.
3. Parallels of caste in history. Social organization in the Middle Ages.
4. Social organization in classical antiquity. Social organization in Egyptian civilization.
4-5. Social evolution in China.
6-7 Caste in India
8. Manu's four castes.
9. Origin of the caste system in India.
10. Caste and the trade guilds.
11. Origin of caste distinctions in the ancient Aryan family.
12 Exclusiveness of primitive peoples a possible cause of caste.
13. Brahminical sway began with the advent of Soma-Haoma priests.
14. Brahmin superiority an essential principle in Hindu organization.
15-16. How did the Brahmin attain his position ?
17. The Rigveda, the poetry of a caste destined for an aristocratic cult.
18. The purpose of sacrifice.
19. Their priestly office made the Brahmins divine.
20. Sacrifice turned into a magic cult.
21. From the Vedic period religion in India moves in an atmosphere of magic.
22. The Brahmins and the nobility.
23. Belief in the efficacy of magic is the source of asceticism.

PAGE SUBJECT

24. The Upanishads, the source of orthodox religious movements in India.
25. The Kshatriya caste is responsible for the theory of Karma.
26. The Brahmins were not eager to accept the progressive ideas of the Kshatriyas.
27. Buddhism and its founder, Gautama Sakyamuni, a Kshatriya.
28-30 Buddha declares caste distinctions futile.
31. Buddhas's intellectual and ethical light shines on all. Caste distinctions observed by the Buddhist laity have no religious significance.
32. Brahmins and the teachings of Buddha.
33. The great Buddhist emperor Asoka.
34-35. The moral teachings of Asoka.
36. Asoka dispenses with Brahminic aid.
37. After Asoka's death Brahminism rises again.
38. The code of Manu declares the Brahmin to be divine.
39. Buddhism during the Pushyamitra dynasty.
39-40. The second stage of the development of the Mahabharata falls into this period.
41. The end of the Pushyamitra dynasty.
42. Buddhism assumes a new form after the Yue-chi conquest of India.
43. Asvagosha, its first expounder.
44-45. His attack on caste in the Vajrasuchi.
46. The end of the reign of Kanishka.
47. Buddhism during the time of his successors. Gupta emperors tolerant towards Buddhism.
48. The Mahabharata in its present form the result of a revision by Brahmins at the Gupta court.
49-50. Influence of Buddha's teachings on the popular mind. The Brahmins put forward a new Kshatriya teacher.
51. Krishna, an incarnation of God, serves to take the place of the Buddha.
52. The Bhagavadgita receives the status of an Upanishad.
53. Caste in the Bhagavadgita.
54. Defence of killing in the Bhagavadgita calls to mind Yuan Chuang's account of Kurukshetra in the Siyuki.

Page **Subject**

55. Philosophical Absolutism and caste.
56-57. Philosophical Absolutism criticised.
58. The theory of three gunas in the Gita.
59. Kumarila's attack on Buddha.
60. The Sankaravijaya on Buddhism.
61. The Brahmin's effort to maintain his supremacy.
62. Brahminism and the partiality for vegetarian diet. Buddhism during the time of King Harsha.
63. Buddhism under the Sena kings.
64. Buddhism under Brahminic sway.
65. Hinduism a proselyting religion.
66. Child marriage a result of the caste system.
67. Fusion of Buddhism and Brahminism.
68-70. Methods employed to maintain the caste system.
70. Samkara.
71. Buddhism in South India.
72. Division of Hindu Society into Brahmin and non-Brahmin classes.
74. The nature and development of religion.
75. Caste the common feature of Hindu religions.
76. Buddhist influence on other religious teachers.
77. The Lingayat sect and reform. Saivism and Buddhism.
78. Bhaktimarga in Vaishnavite cults.
79. The earliest Vaishnavite sect.
80. Jainism and Buddhism.
81. Art a tangible way in which religion shows its influence on civilization.
82. Caste in Vaishnavism. Ramanuja and caste.
83. Caste in the teaching and life of Ramananda.
85. Hinduism during the Mohamedan conquest.
86 The earliest Moslem invaders waged war against Buddhism and Brahminism.
87. The contact of the monotheism of Islam with Vaishnavism.
88. Husain Shah's attempt to reconcile the religious differences of the Hindu and Mussulman communities.
89. Akbar's attitude towards Hinduism.
90-91. Chaitanya and caste.
92-93. Buddhism and the Vaishnavite movement in Bengal.
94. The Mohamedan conquest of Bengal.

PAGE	SUBJECT
95.	Aurangazib threatens Hinduism.
96.	Sivajee the patron of Hinduism.
97.	Caste among the Mohamedans of Upper India.
98-99.	Christianity and caste distinctions.
100.	Ram Mohan Roy and the Brahma Samaj.
101.	The development of the Brahma Samaj under various leaders.
102.	The Arya Samaj.
104.	The Vedanta of Sri Ramakrishna and Swami Vivekananda.
105.	Theosophic Hinduism.
106.	The British administration and caste.
108.	Education under the British administration.
109.	National education.
111.	Nationalists and the caste system.
112.	The influence of the caste system on the country's political life.
113.	The influence of the caste system on the country's intellectual life.
114.	Attempted defence of caste on scientific grounds.
115.	The classification of mankind into races.
117.	Purity of blood a myth.
118.	Caste and eugenics.
120.	Men are fundamentally alike and therefore equal.
121.	This equality implies equality of opportunity.
122.	Self-development must be open to all.
123.	The fallacy of the theory of the four Varnas demonstrated on physiological and sociological grounds.
124.	Brahminic philosophy is based on the belief in soul and Karma.
125.	The caste system has not solved the problem between capital and labour.
127.	The system of castes and Plato's Republic.
128.	The origin of caste is not economic but mystic and occult.
130.	Manu on the supremacy of Brahmins.
131.	Caste the mainstay of the Hindu religion,
132.	The system of castes a part of the Hindu conception of the Universe.
133.	The Hindu doctrine of Karma.

PAGE	SUBJECT
134	The doctrine of Karma fails to separate the human from the animal kingdom.
135.	The doctrine of transmigration and the belief in a soul.
136.	Belief in a soul has no basis in modern science.
138.	The phenomenon of life.
139.	The thinking soul (Atman) and the principle of life (Prana).
140.	How people come by their various beliefs.
142.	Personality a compound of body and mind.
143.	Death does not end all.
144.	Man a component of the community of human beings.
145.	The negation of a soul leads to the denial of a creating *deus extra mundum*.
146-147.	The assumption of a Providence is not a scientific hypothesis.
148.	Man is not evil by nature.
149.	Every system of morality is a body of imperfect social generalizations.
150-151.	Man's baser emotions spring from the need of food and interests connected with reproduction.
152.	Civilization is the result of mutual aid and utility.
153-154.	The denial of soul and God does not imply a denial of all religion.
155-156.	Progress in religion consists in a reconciliation between religion and science.
157.	Progress comprises tendencies and movements that make for a better society.
158.	The spirit of nationality is no better than the spirit of caste.
159.	The consciousness of the unity of all mankind makes for beautiful and happy lives.

ERRATA.

PAGE	LINE	READ	FOR
4	8	hereditary	hereditory
11	31	ancient	aucient
16	4	Vedas	vedas
16	33	diminution	diminition
31	26	occasion	occassion
32	37	Saddharma	Saddharna
36	19	right way	rightway
42	31	Sanskrit	sanscrit
46	12	*varna*	*vama*
46	20	conformation	confirmation
47	24	dealings	deelings
47	30	abhorrent	abhonent
48	12	underwent	under went
50	31	Panini	Paunini
53	18	serenity	screnity
53	27	perfection	prefection
56	29	philosophies	philosophics
57	28	*tāt tvam asi*	*tatvamasit*
59	28	Kumarila	Kamarila
64	18	shepherd	shephered
66	22	Rarhi	Rashi
72	1	royal	Royal
78	28	poisonous	poisonouss
83	43	sticklers	stcklers
90	15	were	was
95	6	conceal	canceal
98	6	number	member
108	27	Philippines	Phillipines
127	42	pursuit of	pursuitof
143	40	nor	not
144	43	individual	ihvidual
157	18	*Weltgeschichte*	*Weltgeschicte*
159	1	the	ths
159	1	by	hy

A STUDY OF CASTE

"The thing we in India have got to think of is this—to remove those social customs and ideals which have generated a want of self-respect and a complete dependence on those above us—a state of affairs which has been brought about entirely by the domination in India of the caste system, and the blind and lazy habit of relying upon the authority of traditions that are incongruous anachronisms in the present age."—Rabindranath Tagore.

It has been rightly said that the highest ideal of sociology lies in the amelioration of social pathology. To this end must therefore be subordinated all antiquarianism and historical investigation. An investigation into the nature and basis of the rule of caste in India cannot but prove a valuable factor for progress. This then is my apology for this study.

Naturally there are some preliminary questions which need to be first considered. Is caste a universal phenomenon common to all civilizations, or is it a phenomenon peculiar to India? What is its relation to similar social divisions, such as guild, clan, class? Some regard the division into castes as common to the majority of ancient nations. In all ancient societies we observe ethnic differences, political parties, professional specializations. Normal to all societies is the antipathy between the patrician and the plebeian, the landlord and the tenant, the rich and the poor. The repugnance of the Brahmin for the Pariah is not different in kind from the repugnance of the master for his scavenger. On the other hand, others emphasise that caste is a thing unique in the history of the world, being essentially a Hindu institution. To be able to decide between these two views we should first define clearly what caste is.

The feature of caste that strikes even the most superficial observer is hereditary specialization. The son of a soldier is a soldier, the son of a blacksmith is a blacksmith, the son of a scavenger is a scavenger. The work a man does is not determined by his aptitude or desire but by his descent. Family and profession are coupled. The son can choose only the profession of the father. It is not only the right but also the duty of a son to follow the avocation of his father. This spirit prevails in a society subject to caste.

Coupled with the hereditary division of labour is the inequality of rights and privileges attached to the various castes. Every caste monopolizes not only certain professions but also certain privileges. By the very fact of one's birth one is exempted from taxes, while another is taxed heavily. In a court of law the former is worth a hundred mohurs, while the latter is worth only ten. The dress which one wears is entirely forbidden to the other. The rank of the group to which one belongs by birth determines one's personal status for good. Inequalities and special privileges form the second feature of caste.

Mutual repulsion between the different groups into which a society subject to caste is divided is a third feature of caste. A man who is under the sway of caste dare not seek a wife outside his traditional circle; he refuses food prepared by other than his congeners and views the contact of strangers as impure and degrading. Wherever caste wields influence, we observe the horror of misalliance, the fear of impure contacts, the mutual exclusiveness between the several groups into which society is divided.

Mutual repulsion, hierarchical organization and hereditary specialization are the three main characteristics of caste. Caste rules a society, if it is divided into a large number of groups, mutually exclusive, hereditarily specialized and hierarchically organised, and if it does not tolerate in principle the commingling of blood, the acquisition of rank and the change of profession.

Guided by this definition of caste we may look through history for examples in which these tendencies characteristic of caste are wholly or partially found. For example, contemporary occidental civilization reveals certain traces of the spirit of caste. The horror of misalliances and the fear of impure contacts are still noticeable. The idea of "equality of birth" surviving in European royalty is surely that of a caste conception. Alliances between members of different social spheres are not very common. Different classes of the population of a country do not freely mix with one another. Certain schools are frequented only by certain classes of the community. These distinctions undoutedly correspond in a large measure to the grades of a hierarchy. Though the laws may not avow the existence of classes, the manners of the people prove their existence. But no one will contend that caste dominates European civilization. All judicial, political and economic reforms of recent times are found even on a superficial examination to be the results of the dominance of the idea of equality. Law no longer hallows such modes of life as remind us of caste. Where the tendencies characteristic of caste still subsist, they are merely survivals.

When we turn to the Middle Ages, the divisions of society are more and more marked. Between the different groups the distances are more marked not only by manners, but also by laws, and the professions are more frequently monopolised by families. Yet the social organization of the Middle Ages does not correspond to the precise definition of caste that has been given above. The difference between caste and the class division of the Middle Ages comes out clearly, when we examine the social characteristics of the Catholic clergy and the feudal lords who then held sway. If the idea of heredity is essential to caste, the Catholic clergy cannot constitute a caste, because the clergy are all celibates. By their very mode of recruitment the clergy indirectly help ideas which are subversive of those underlying caste. A slave may become a pope and the son of a commoner may become greater than a king. A great distance likewise separates feudal government from caste rule. The fundamental principle of the former is that "the condition of the land determines the man," a principle quite contrary to that of caste, in which one's status is determined by one's birth. Conquest or contract may render one the possessor of a land, and this will raise one in the social scale. The possessor of many fiefs may be the vassal of some and the lord of others, which would make it difficult to define clearly his social rank. Such a system cannot in strictness be regarded as a hierarchy. Again, a feudal lord lived on his lands and governed on his own account a certain number of men who depended only on him. The feudal system is therefore characterized more by a collection of individual despotisms than by a superposition of different groups. It lends itself to individualism, but does not cut up society, as caste does, into small groups which repel one another.

In classical antiquity the city was for a long time marked by a strict hierarchy. Leaving aside slaves, religious, legal and political inequalities separated the plebeian from the patrician. Hereditary specialization was not unknown. In Greek history we often meet with families of physicians or families of priests. The very names of the four Ionian tribes at Athens are the names of professions. The cult of ancestors stood in the way of the several groups forming the city mixing together. Yet it was the mission of the ancient city to surmount this tendeney. Hereditory specialization was an exception rather than the rule. Hierarchical organization did not develop into the superposition of mutually repelling groups. In fact, so long as the city remained a collection of *gens*, the inferiors did not form separate groups; slaves or dependants belonged to the family and formed part of one corporate body. Later when an independent common people came into being, they imposed on the city new groupings which displaced the old divisions and forced the citizens to mix. United into demes, the classes, following their fortunes or armaments, could not remain grouped into clans. Gradually the equality of rights and privileges was won. The work of reformers helped to remove the traces left by the primitive divisions. Thus, even in antiquity, occidental civilization was opposed to the spirit of caste.

Older than classical civilization is Egyptian civilization. Not infrequently it is asserted that Egyptian civilization represented a type subject to caste regime. Herodotus tells us that Egyptians were divided into seven *gens*: priests, warriors, cowherds, swineherds, merchants, interpreters and pilots. Only the priests and warriors enjoyed marks of distinction; special lands were reserved for them, and they were exempted from all taxes. When a priest died, his place was taken by his son. Warriors alone could follow the profession of arms, which passed from father to son. Diodorus represents this hereditary specialization not only as a custom but as a practice enforced by laws. At first sight these ancient writers seem to be confirmed by modern researches. The trilingual inscription on the Rosetta stone speaks of sacred, military and royal lands. Some documents testify to certain privileges specially reserved for the military and sacerdotal classes. On the other hand, a number of inscriptions prove that there were dynasties belonging to all strata of society. Division of labour does not seem to have been clearly defined. Sacerdotal, military and civil functions did not exclude each other. Specialization was not therefore absolute. The Egyptian tendency was rather to accumulate than to separate employments. There is positive proof that no man was confined for life to the profession of his father. The example of the son of a poor scribe rising to be the primate of the Western Gate shows that the social hierarchy was not petrified. Pharoah could, by granting lands or revenues, create nobles. Intermarriage was the rule, except between the swine-herds and the other classes. There is nothing which enables us to assert that the spirit of division and mutual repulsion, so characteristic of caste, dominated Egyptian society. If a system of prohibitions isolated for a long time its elementary groups, the administrative organization tended to efface the spontaneous divisions of the population. The Nile necessitated a unity, a common culture, which removed the mutual repugnance between the classes or tribes. Whatever might be the reason, the Egyptian civilization did not develop the invincible resistance to unification which characterises caste regime. If the power of democracy resisted the development of caste in European civilization, so did a powerful monarchy hinder the development of caste in Egyptian civilization.

In China social evolution took place on lines roughly parallel to those elsewhere. The traditional Chinese social system recognised four main classes below the priest-emperor. The Chinese emperor, the "son of Heaven," was himself a high priest, his chief duty being sacrificial. It is not without struggle that the ruler attained this position by breaking up tradition. The leading class consists of the literate men of China, but it is not a caste in the Indian sense. Unlike the Brahmins the mandarins, the name by which the literate class is known, are not born, but they become so by education. Members of all classes of the communinty can become mandarins by education and examination. The Chinese mandarin is the product of hard mental work. The son of a mandarin has no prescriptive right to succeed his father. It has been the custom in China from the earliest times to divide one's landed property among all the sons. There has therefore never been in China great landlords, renting their land to tennants. Soldiers and labourers have been recruited from the impecunious masses of the town population owning scarcely any property at all. The life of a soldier is despised in China. The complexities of the written language of China enabled the mandarinate to prevail, but the mandarins do not form a caste.

Now when we turn to investigate the question of caste in India, we tread on different ground. We find the three essentials of caste in full swing. Nowhere has the suppression of individuality and hereditary specialization been pushed so far as in India. Though the number of professions may not be as large as in any advanced country of modern Europe, yet each grand profession is divided into a number of subdivisions, which in reality correspond to no professional distinction. In the majority of cases what distinguishes one caste from its congeners is that it abstains from certain methods, does not utilize the same materials, or does not produce the same articles. For example, fishermen are divided into different castes according to the appliances they employ, or according to the fish they catch; potters are divided into two castes according as they work standing and make large pots, or turn the wheel sitting and make small pots. Different castes of domestic servants have each their proper employment, and a servant of one caste emphatically declines to do the work of another caste. From top to toe plurality of functions is interdicted in principle in Hindu society. The work one has to do is assigned once for all by his descent. No one has the right to change his function. Hereditary specialization is the rule and it has been so from a remote past. But we should also note that this system of hereditary specialization has much greater flexibility than appears at first sight. For example, all kinds of professions have been open to the Brahmins at all times. Far from confining themselves to the study of the sacred books they have acted as kings, soldiers, merchants, cooks, agriculturists and labourers. Even their superiority has opened out to them more possibilities than to common mortals. Manu declares that a Brahmin should always be regarded as a great divinity, "whatever may be the profession to which he may be devoted." The higher the caste the more numerous the occupations open to it. Following the example of the Brahmins the members of the other castes have given up in some cases the occupations enjoined for them in the codes and taken to other professions. In many cases the change of profession is regarded legally as illicit and involves a social degradation. A peculiarity of the flexibility in relation to hereditary specialization is that it is collective rather than individual. No individual is allowed to renounce the profession of his father to satisfy his own natural aptitude and inclination. It is rather groups that detach themselves from the whole to take to new professions, but within each group the rule is that the son follows the profession of his father. The individual who ventures to transgress this rule is *ipso facto* a rebel and an outcaste. The fact that, when a group changes its profession, it seeks to justify the change by a legend which exculpates it from the censure of public opinion, indicates that to the conscience of the Hindu attachment to the profession of the ancestors appeals as a duty, from which he ought not to swerve except for sacred reasons.

Passing from hereditary specialization to hierarchical organization, nowhere do we observe such marked distinctions as in Hindu society. The castes and their subdivisions are numberless. Above all is the Brahmin, although the prestige of a Brahmin may not be the same in all conditions. "A Brahmin", says Manu, "be he ignorant or learned, is a great divinity." The absolute superiority of the Brahmin is as uucontested as the absolute inferiority of the Pariah. Between these two extremes are comprehended the innumerable castes, each with its rank and prerogatives. The rank of a caste is determined by such considerations as purity of blood, fidelity to the ancestral profession, abstention from interdicted foods and drinks. The sacred texts also define with almost mathematical precision the differences between the several castes. But in practice the criterion which settles the dignity of a caste is the esteem in which the Brahmin holds it, that is, the kind of relationship as regards receiving gifts, food and drink from its members by those of the Brahmin caste. It is the conformity with the Brahminic ideas that confers rank. In the eyes of the orthodox Hindu any other caste than his own is in a sense impure. In South India when a Brahmin enters a Parachery water mixed with cowdung is sprinkled after he leaves it, just as they do after a corpse is removed from a Hindu home. No wonder that between the several castes into which Hindu society is split up there is mutual repulsion.

This sentiment of repulsion is exhibited specially in the matter of commensality and marriage. Therefore the fear of pollution is the basis of the sentiment of repulsion. The fear of pollution drives the Hindu to isolate himself for eating. A proverb says: "For three Kanouj Brahmins thirty fires are needed," and another says: "For a dozen Rajputs thirteen kitchens are needed." These scruples are observed not only by the high castes but also by all from top to bottom. Marriage outside one's caste is rigorously interdicted. Caste is rigidly endogamous, although it seems to be coupled with internal exogamy. This endogamous character isolates the castes and tends to shut them out for ever from one another. Although anthropologists have shown that in spite of this restriction the mixtures are numerous, yet in the eyes of the Hindu a pure marriage is only one contracted between the members of the same caste. A marriage outside caste entails a greater degradation than a change of occupation. Hence the fissiparous tendency may be considered to be inherent in Hindu society.

Though Manu is quoted as saying that there are only four castes and that there is no fifth, this *chaturvarna* has never been more than an ideal. The Jataka tales, ascribed to Gautama Sakyamuni of the seventh century B. C. already refer to a multiplicty of castes. Jolly quotes from Sanskrit literature more than forty names of *jatis*, which bear no correspondence to the subdivisions of the primitive four *varnas*. It is difficult to determine in the existing castes the actual descendants of the four traditional castes: Brahmins who devote themselves only to study and sacrifice, Kshatriyas who only fight, Vaisyas who only trade, and Sudras who only serve others. The castes fall into two great divisions, the pure and the impure. A great gulf separates the pure from the impure. But the impure castes also have many divisions of social rank, among whom there is much emulation; each group, though despised by the Brahmin, aspires to be more respectable than its neighbour. Even the lowest take a pride in their caste and are exclusive. No better proof is needed of the existence of a mutual repulsion between the constituent parts of Hindu society.

Caste, as represented by one or the other of its three characteristics, made its appearance in all civilizations. In most countries the transmission of profession from father to son was common at one time or other. We may notice a parallel between the sacerdotal class of Levites among the Hebrews and the Brahmins of India. In the most unified peoples avowed even to democracy there have been in their primitive stages divisions which naturally excluded one another. Thus the elements of comparison between the caste system of India and the civilizations of other countries are not lacking. But it is in the Hindu caste system that we find the synthesis of the elements found everywhere, the completion of the traces visible everywhere, the unique blossoming of universal tendencies. India may therefore be righty characterised as the special land in which caste rules in all its vigour and bloom. Bharatavarsha, the land of the black antelope, is the special preserve of the system of castes.

What then are the origins of this institution, which exists only in India? At this distance of time it may not be possible to say precisely how the system of castes originated. Yet by way of elimination we may discover what causes have not played a part. At the very commencement we may reject the theory that ascribes the origin of castes to the cunning policy of ambitious priests, who modelled Hindu society wholly to their advantage. The impartial study of institutions has shown that few of them are based on mere charlatanry. The complex and long-standing character of the system of castes makes it improbable that the system could have been a deliberate invention. A theory, closely akin but equally preposterous, is the one that ascribes the design of the caste system to Brahminism for the purpose of developing *satvic* qualities whose acquisition is posited as the soul of all progress. To make the organisation of Hindu society depend solely on the will of the Brahmins would be to exaggerate the part played by voluntary creation in the growth of human society, although it must be granted that caste has served as a bulwork to preserve much of the Brahmin's heritage from decay and dissolution.

Attempts have been made to liken the Hindu castes to the trade-guilds of medieval Europe. From the remotest antiquity professional differences have exerted great influence on the life of the Hindu. The utility and the dignity of the occupation followed by a caste is determinative of its rank. Each caste or group of castes may be viewed as corresponding to a step of progress by which man increases his sway over things. May not therefore the Hindu hierarchy respond in a general way to the phases of industrial evolution? The pressure of industry gives rise to the multiplicity of professions and brings about the growth of corporations as a consequence. Why should not Hindu corporations have responded to the same needs as the Germanic corporations? Castes might therefore be regarded as petrified guilds. Now, we could speak of a caste as a guild only if to every different profession corresponded a different caste and *vice versa*.

But the members of one and the same caste often follow different professions. Many castes are named not only after their professions but also after their localities. In some cases a caste has no relation to industrial life. The worshippers of the same saint or the followers of the same prophet (such as Kabirpanthis and Dadupanthis) form a closed group. In such cases the caste is born of a sect and not of a professional corporation. In some respects there is a resemblance between the guilds of the Middle Ages and the Hindu castes. The guilds of the Middle Ages were not wholly industrial or economical corporations. Each guild formed a fraternity with its common chest for mutual help, its chapel, its feasts, its cult, its jurisdiction. It exercised supervision not only on the qualities of the goods produced by its members but also on the conduct of the latter. A guild formed, as it were, a large family, and it was in relation to its function as a family that it instituted its cult, its sacrifices, its common repast, its vault. It is here we find the spirit of the *gens* in the professional guilds, and this is the feature that makes a medieval guild resemble a caste. But in these guilds are found none of the three features peculiar to caste. The guilds never forbade a man to marry outside his own guild, nor did they object to take apprentices from other guilds or from the outside community. Members of different guilds ate together and in the assertion and defence of their common interests the various guilds joined together, but the tendency of caste is to split up into subdivisions of a mutually exclusive character. Membership in a guild was open to all workers in a certain trade, and every man was free to apprentice his son to a trade different from his own. Though cases of this kind were not general, because oral tradition was the only mode of conserving ideas and practices and it was inevitable that the father should transmit to his son the secret of his profession, yet they ocurred with sufficient frequency to show that occupation was not in the days of the guilds determined by caste and that caste divisions were not maintained by professional differences. Further, the guilds did much to improve the industries they represented, but can we say that caste has been favourable to the development of the arts and industries of the Hindus ? Caste organization may be utilized for the various purposes for which a guild might serve. But to assert that caste organization is to the Hindu, his club, his trade union, his benefit society, his philanthropic society and so forth is more a fancy than a fact. If, as has been contended, the natural history of industry could furnish the key to the hierarchical organization of Hindu society, how should we account for the position of the Brahmin at the summit of the whole edifice? Do the methods of incantation and sacrifice employed by the Brahmin correspond to any advanced phase of industrial progress? The prestige of the Brahmin may not be measurable by materialistic criteria; but only material considerations have weight, when any matter is examined from an industrial and economic standpoint. If hereditary specialization appeals to the soul of the Hindu as an obligatory duty, we must look for its reason not in economic tendencies but in the idea of *taboo* so common among primitive peoples and in the theocracy at the basis of the system of castes. Just as certain objects are *taboo* for certain families, so are certain professions interdicted to some and prescribed for others. A religious idea sways the industrial organization of Hindu society.

The mutual repulsion between the several castes has led some indologists to look for the origin of caste in the ancient Aryan family. The ancient Aryan family was essentially a religious association bringing together for the same cult around a common hearth the *gens* of the same blood. The desire for the continuity and purity of the cult was the source of many prescriptions which were laid down for its members. For example, the repast, which was the product of the sacred fire, was the external sign of the unity of the family; hence the interdiction in primitive society of partaking the repast of a stranger. Similarly, in the laws relating to marriage, religious scruples swayed in the ancient family organizations. It was in the name of sacred law that the patrician of pure race remained faithful to his ancient religion avoiding alliance with the impure plebeians of mixed origin, destitute of family rites. Between the castes of India similar barriers exist as regards eating and marriage. May not also the prescriptions and prohibitions relating to connubium and commensality in Hindu society be due to the religious conceptions peculiar to the Aryans? May not caste be a lineal descendant of the Aryan family? Many facts are opposed to this view of the origin of caste. The beliefs and practices which are regarded as peculiar to the Aryans are found also among other peoples. Fear of impurity of blood and scruples about touch are common to almost all primitive peoples. The Semites also had special prescriptions and prohibitions about commensality and connubium. The sacrificial repast among the Semites was essentially a feast of relatives. The sacred repast united the faithful not only to God but also to one another; it gave to them the same flesh and made the same blood flow in them. The prescriptions of caste as regards repast may be traced to ideas common to all primitive peoples but that does not prove an Aryan basis. Nor is the endogamy which separates the Hindu castes from one another peculiar only to the tribes of the Aryan race. If the rules of caste agree largely with the old laws relating to *gens*, on one important point there is an essential difference. The members of a *gens* are interdicted from marrying among one another, but caste prescribes this. The former is as rigorously exogamic as the latter is endogamic. The spirit of caste can not therefore be said to have originated from the family. Further, forms of marriage which appear most opposed to endogamic practices, such as marriage by capture, are in reality reconcilable with endogamy. Before contracting marriage the captured woman is first adapted into the family. Endogamy appears therefore much more general than was believed at first. Like the Hindu castes many tribes of very different races are endogamous, while their sections are exogamous. Hence the scruples of the Hindu concerning marriage do not necessarily prove the Aryan descent of the Hindu caste. All that we can say is that the spirit common to all primitive societies which exclude one another owing to religious scruples has survived to the present day in the castes of India.

It is not improbable that the family exclusiveness characteristic of primitive peoples lies at the bottom of the mutual repulsion observed between the various Hindu castes. The emigrants who called themselves "Aryas" probably settled at first in the Iranian plateau. A comparison of the language of the Veda with that of the Iranian Avesta proves that these languages are dialects of one and the same older language. Entire passages of the Veda may be converted into good specimens of the Avesta by mere phonetic modifications. The most striking characteristics of the period when the ancestors of the Iranians and the Vedic Aryans lived together appear to be the development of the worship of fire (*agni*) combined with magic and the introduction of the soma drink at sacrifices. The ritual of *Soma-Haoma* which came into vogue gave birth to a clergy of its own. By a slow progress the members of certain clans, better provided than others with technical knowledge in rites and formulas, became the masters of the sacrificial altar and the recognised intermediaries between gods and men. Just as among the ancient Romans the pontifices became powerful and influential owing to their knowledge of all the details of sacrificial ceremonies, so did also the masters of the sacrificial altar among the ancestors of the Vedic Aryans and the ancient Iranians form themselves into a special priestly class. The gradual formation of a priestly class and the respect it showed to the various professions followed by the members of the community gradually led up to the division of society into classes. The existence of classes in ancient Indo-Iranian society may be surmised from the existence of the four *pishtras* among the ancient Iranians, namely, the Athravas or priests, the Rathaestas or warriors, the Vastriyas-Fshoyants, or chiefs of families, and the Huites or manual labourers. The four *pishtras* of the Avesta represent only classes and not castes in the Hindu sense of the word. The reformation of Zoroaster appears to have wiped out any differences that might have existed between the various classes.

A company of the more adventurous spirits among the Athravas appears to have set out to secure for themselves new domains among the neighbouring Dravidians. These Dravidians were not a primitive people, but tilled the ground, worked in metals, traded with foreign countries, possessed forts and chariots. They had among them aristocracy and serfs. The former held all the land and possessed all the wealth of the country. The latter cultivated the land for their masters, but did not hold it themselves. The Aryan immigrants came among the Dravidians as astrologers and sorcerers carrying with them their Indra-Agni cult, but they seem to have brought with them few women or none at all. They influenced the *elite* among the darker Dravidians, established themselves as priests and took women according to their needs. They found themselves cut off from their original stock partly by the distance and partly by the alliances they had contracted. By marrying women from the Dravidians they had to some extent modified their original type, but a certain pride of blood remained in them. When they had bred females enough to serve their purposes and to establish a distinct *jus connubii*, they closed their ranks to further intermixture of blood. When they did this, they became a caste like the castes of the present day. The old term for caste is *varna*, colour, which implies purity of descent, and it is the fear of the Aryans being merged in the Dravidians as an indistingnishable mass that led to the proscribing of exogamy. According to Fick marriages between members of the same family were of common occurrence in the ancient period. "The union of men and women descended from the same ancestor and of blood relations in the third and fourth degrees is represented as a general practice." As the immigrants only took women but did not give them, complete amalgamation with the older inhabitants did not take place. It is not unlikely that the Athrava immigrants formed an esoteric community which kept their knowledge as an inherited treasure and that their occupation therefore became hereditary. In insisting on a standard of purity they introduced into the Dravidian society a division into classes on a basis similar to the *pishtras* of their original home. The general resemblance between the *pishtras* of the ancient Iranians and the *chaturvarnas* spoken of in the *Purushasuktam* of the Rigveda is very close. Though in the Brahminic tradition the Vaisyas are described as agriculturists and merchants, yet in the literature of the Buddhists they are ordinarily called *grihapathis* or heads of families. Further among the Iranians the admission of an individual into the community of the higher classes was marked by the investiture of the sacred thread, a ceremony similar to the one obtaining among the *dvijas* of Hindu society. We may therefore infer with great probability that the Brahmins are descended from the Soma-Haoma priests of the ancient Indo-Iranian community.

A society can not long be divided into closed groups without accepting some sort of hierarchy. For example, when the Israelites became broken up into tribes, some were despised, and others, like Ephraim, were treated with respect. The formation of classes in Hindu society gradually led to a hierarchical organization. The chief features of this organization reveal to us the mode of its growth. The keystone of the hierarachical organization of Hindu society is the universally recognised primacy of the Brahmin caste. Not only does the Brahmin officiate in most of the ceremonies of the Hindu family, but also takes the place of the *pitris* (ancestors) in funeral repasts and offerings to the manes of ancestors. The superiority of the Brahmin is one of the essential principles of the social organization of the Hindus; it is, in short, the most certain characteristic of Hinduism. It is indeed true that everywhere the sacredotal class possesses special privileges and often holds the first rank. But rarely does it reign uncontested and by its sole power. Most often it has to reckon with a secular power, which limits the extent of its privileges and sometimes gradually reduces its influence. For example, in Egypt, as Herodotus tells us, the priests held the highest rank, had special privileges, were exempt from all taxes, and lands were specially reserved for them. The temple priests formed a class by themselves, not mixing with the people engaged in civil work. But the sovereign had complete control over temples and he placed his creatures at their head. All estates in the realm were under the domination of the royal sovereign. Similarly in the Middle Ages the spiritual power in spite of its great influence did not succeed in subordinating the temporal power. During the Catholic theocracy the kings ruled by divine right and they were all powerful. On the other hand, in the Brahminic theocracy, it is the priests that remain at the pinnacle. Among the Hindus the sacerdotal class has become so firmly established and its influence has so deeply permeated the community that it has been able to prescribe, under the sanction of religion, a code of elaborate prescriptions on domestic and personal conduct which is accepted by all as the ideal, the relative conformity to which settles the status of every group of the Hindu society from top to bottom

How did the Brahmin attain this position? It was not by organized effort. There is as much lack of unity among the Brahmins as among the others. All Brahmins do not obey a single superior as do, for example, the Jesuits. Nor can they be said to constitute what may be called a clergy. There is nothing in Brahminism which has the semblance of an organisation. It has never had councils for settling disputed points or electing a superior. The Brahmins have never lived together in convents, submitting to the same discipline, as did the Buddhist *bhikshus*. The Brahmins are priests without a church; they have no commandments to obey nor a pontiff to venerate. The great article of faith of Brahminism is the sacrosanct character of the born priest. Though according to the sacred texts the young Brahmin has to go through a novitiate extending over many years, learning the vedas from the revered mouth of his teacher, yet the Brahmin is born and not made. His rights and privileges are not the price of his knowledge or virtue, but the prestige of his blood. Since it is birth that confers dignity on the Brahmin, all Brahmins are equal. Just as Brahminism has no church, so it is also a religion without dogmas. It is defined rather by rites than by dogmas, by practices than by ideas. All can enter it and none need go out of it. Its pantheism easily embraces all creations of polytheism; the most divergent deities can find a place in it by becoming *avataras*, relations, or servants of the traditional deities. The essential of Brahminism is the veneration of the Brahmin and the cow, coupled with the observance of certain rules as to inter marriage and interdining, the wearing of marks on the forehead, and the worship of the Brahminic gods. It is therefore closed only to the *mlechchas*, as those are dubbed who do not accept the supremacy of the Brahmin and the rules of caste. It is not the power of organization that gives strength to the priests of Hinduism. It is the preponderating part that religion plays in the life of the Hindu that gives power to the priests. For the Hindu every natural habit and duty has a religious significance. It is impossible for him to draw a distinction between the profane and the sacred. His religion defines for him his customary rule of every day life, his social identity, his whole status and the signs by which he may be known and described. A man is not a Hindu, because he inhabits India, or belongs to any particular race or state but because he is a Brahminist. "This omnipresence of the religious sanction and the rigidity which it imparts to diversity elsewhere susceptible of diminition or effacement is not only the most prominent feature of the social organization of India, but is also peculiar to the latter marking it out as distinct from any other civilization in the world."

Religion is born of a feeling of dependence on unknown factors in the endeavour towards self-preservation. The manner in which this feeling is interpreted depends on the way in which man understands his own nature, his personality. To interpret dream life the primitive man imagined the presence inside a living animal or man exhibiting spontaneous motion a subtle animal or man called the soul (*atman*). The soul was supposed to enter the body at birth and quit it at death and to form the active agent in the movements of the various motor organs. Wherever motion was perceived, a soul or ghost was supposed to be present. The whole universe was peopled with spirits; those favorable to man were called *devas* and those harmful to man were called *asuras*. The deities of the Vedic hymns were spirits corresponding to the forces of nature. They moved in the heavens and ruled the course of the sun and stars, they rode on the storms, moved in the waters, and lived in the friendly fire. The human mind is incapable of expressing its relation to the deities which it has fashioned in any other way than by attributing to them a nature similar to its own. Man simply sees himself, his nature, his human nature, the best and the worst that he knows, projected on to the clouds. No wonder that the Vedic gods possess human attributes. Sacrifices of burnt flesh and intoxicating soma drink were offered to them to persuade them to satisfy the wishes of the worshippers.

The oldest religious document of India is a collection of hymns, called the Rig Veda. In the initial enthusiasm of discovery these hymns were, for a long time, believed to be the spontaneous effusions of a primitive pastoral people. But now most indologists are convinced that in the large majority of hymns we have a liturgy of a sacerdotal and artificial character, whose origin from a long past is clearly indicated by its obscure and stereo-typed phraseology. In their present form the majority of hymns appear made for a cult and not for any of the acts of the ordinary religious life. They seem designed above all for those great ceremonies in which was poured the sacred liquor *soma*. We rarely find in them the expression of a simple religious sentiment or popular belief, they form the poetry of a caste destined for an aristocratic cult. The care with which this poetry designedly avoids all precise conceptien of gods proves that it is not popular but sacerdotal. The personality of the deity seems to play only a secondary role. The centre of religion is in the religious act itself and not in the divinity which is its object. Even if all the sacred literature has not emanated directly from the Brahmin caste, it is through their intermediary that it has been transmitted. We can therefore be confident that the doctrine relating to the sacrifice as embodied in it has originated from that caste.

In the beginning sacrifices were probably offered with a view to avert the wrath of the gods whom men feared. But in later times sacrifices were regarded as a means of communication between man and gods. As fire is both celestial and terrestrial and also passes between the earth and the heavens in the form of lightning (*garutman*), Agni, the god of fire, kindled in every sacrifice, was supposed to act as the middleman between men and gods and bear the oblation to the gods. If sacrifice could be a means of communicating with the gods, it would not be impossible for man to enter into economic relations with them. If man could offer the gods something that would please them, it should also be possible for the gods to give man in return what he might desire. Thus in due course sacrifice developed into a kind of bartering with the gods. "*Dehi me, dadami te*—I give in order that you may give" is the burden of almost every vedic hymn, and is the explicit or implied reason of every Vedic sacrifice. From the conception of sacrifice as a kind of barter easily arose the idea that sacrifice could not only buy the gods, but that the gods could, even against their will, be coerced by means of sacrifice to do what man desired. As Prof. Sylvain Levi has pointed out in his *La Doctrine du Sacrifice dans les Brahmanas*, the sacrifice which regulates the relation of man to the gods, is a mechanical act, operating by its own spontaneous power, and the magic art of the priest brings out what is hidden in the bosom of nature. The hymn to the gods uttered by the priest at the sacrifice was known as the *Brahman*. In course of time it came to signify a magical incantation, possessing magical power. Every letter, syllable and word of the incantation, possessed a supernatural potency. Finally it became the creative source and primal cause of all things. Says the *Satapatha Brahmanam*: "The creator through austerity created first the incantation, the *Brahman* or *Veda*, therefore the *Brahman* is the foundation of everything here." As the *Brahman* or incantation became the personification of all creative power and of all knowledge, so likewise the chanters of the *Brahman*, the Brahmanas, came to be considered as the very personifications of all revealed lore and of all divine powers. It is the belief that the Brahmins, as the guardians of the sacrifice, possessed the knowledge and power to open and shut to man the approach to the gods, which forms the profound source of the privileges of the Brahmin caste. It is not mere descent that forms the reason of the Brahmin's superiority. For, like the Brahmin the Kshatriya also claims to be of pure blood. In the *Ambatta Sutta* Sakyamuni claims for the Kshatriya superiority on the ground of purity of descent. "So it is clear," he says, "whether you regard it from the male, or from the female side, that it is the Kshatriyas who are the best people, and the Brahmanas their inferiors." Similarly in the *Vanaparva* of the *Mahabharata* Brahma Sanatkumara says: "The Kshatriya is the best of those among the folk who put their trust in lineage." It is the nature of the function reserved for the Brahmin that determined the prestige of his blood.

Through their priestly office the Brahmins came to be divine. The operations needed to act on the will of the gods were complex, involving innumerable manipulations and recitations and could not be effected without special training. But it was not this training alone that tended to raise the Brahmin in the estimation of the other Hindus. According to primitive ideas the sacrifice intended to put man in communication with the gods also invested the man who performed the sacrifice with a special nature: the sacrificer himself became a "sacred" being. In the words of the *Satapatha Brahmanam* "he who is consecrated draws nigh to the gods and becomes one of the deities." "All formulas of the consecration are *audgrabhana* (elevatory), since he who is consecrated elevates himself (*udgrabh*) from this world to the world of the gods. He elevates himself by these formulas." "He who is consecrated becomes both Vishnu and a sacrificer; for when he is consecrated, he is Vishnu, and when he sacrifices, he is the sacrificer." The means by which the sacrificer passes from the human to the divine is a simulation of a new birth. He is sprinkled with water as a symbol of seed. He feigns to be an embryo, and shuts himself in a special hut, which represents the womb. Under his robe he wears a belt and over it the skin of a black antelope; the belt stands for the navel string, and the robe and the black antelope skin represent the inner and outer membranes (the amnion and the chorion) in which the embryo is wrapt. He must not scratch himself with his nails or a stick, because he is an embryo and an embryo scratched with nails or a stick will die. If he moves about in the hut, it is because the foetus moves about in the womb. If he keeps his fists doubled up, it is because an unborn babe does the same. If in bathing he puts off the black antelope skin but retains his robe, it is because the child is born with the amnion but not with the chorion. By these practices he acquires, in addition to his old natural and mortal body, a new body that is sacramental and immortal, invested with superhuman powers, encircled with an aureole of fire. Thus, by a new birth, a regeneration of his carnal nature, man becomes divine. The habitual performance of the sacrifice gives the sacrificer a second nature and makes him one with those divinities whom he puts in communication with men. The saturation of the human nature with the divine nature could be so deep that the sacred character of the sacrificer remains attached to him not only during his life but is also transmitted to his descendants; the divine nature, having passed into the blood, becomes a property of the stock. Thus have come into being the Brahmins, the priests by birth, the "supermen" of Hinduism, whom the Atharvana Veda hails as the "kinsmen of the gods." All Brahmins are therefore equal.

In principle the Brahmin originally discharged the function of preventing the malign powers from obstructing the aim pursued by the sacrificer (*Yajamana*). But little by little in virtue of his possession of the efficacious words he extended the field of his activity, and finally made the cult into a sort of magic. Thus it became possible at a later stage to append without any opprobrium the formulas of sorcery to the Sama Veda, which, in virtue of its musical character, has been described as the most august of the Vedas. If certain passages of the Rig Veda express horror of sorcery, it is not that the Rig Veda finds sorcery morally reprehensible, but sees in it a dangerous rival. The knowledge of the sacred rites proved a powerful but delicate weapon in the hands of the Brahmin and placed the welfare of those that paid him at his mercy. Religion was concentrated in the person of the priest and the laity were pushed aside. Thus arose the distinction of men into two classes, sacred and profane. That commensality between two individuals creates a close connection, that community of aliments produces identity of nature, is a universal idea among primitive peoples, and forms the foundation of one of the most important forms of sacrifice, called the communal sacrifice. It is this idea that has resulted in the interdiction of all commensality between the members of the different castes as well as the scruples about purity of blood and promiscuity of marriage, while the idea of purification of the fleshly abode of the soul by a new magical birth (*upanayāna*) gave rise to the idea of untouchability.

From the Vedic period religion moves in India in an atmosphere of magic. The priests are entirely magicians. The knowledge of the *mantras* and the sacrificial *tantras* enabled the Brahmins to dominate the people of India. A well-known sanskrit verse says, *daivadhinam jagatsarvam, mantradhinam tudaivatam; tanmantram brahmanadhinam, brahmana mamadevata.* The world is subject to the gods, and the gods are subject to the sacrificial *mantras*; and the *mantras* themselves are in the hands of the Brahmins; hence the Brahmins are the real gods, though they live on this earth. Similarly says the *Satapatha Brahmanam*: "Verily there are two kinds of gods; for, indeed, the gods are the gods; and the Brahmins who have studied and teach the sacred lore are the human gods. The sacrifice is of two kinds; oblations constitute the sacrifice to the gods; and gifts to the priests that to the human gods, the Brahmins who have studied and teach the sacred lore." If the belief in the mysterious efficacy of the sacrifice gave preeminence to the Brahmin, the development of that supremacy was due largely to the ambition and selfishness of those who profited by it. The system of castes being profitable to them, the Brahmins fostered and turned it to their own advantage. The sacerdotal caste employed its intellect to turn to account the religious instincts of the people and to deepen and extend their hold on their minds. How else could we account for the customs and practices now obtaining among the Hindus? The orthodox Sudra venerates the Brahmin to such an extent that he will not cross the shadow of a Brahmin. Many of them take a vow not to touch any food in the morning before drinking *vipracharanamrita*, that is, the water in which the toe of a Brahmin has been dipped. The pride of the Brahmin is such that he does not bow to the images of the gods worshipped in a Sudra's house, though the officiating priests may be Brahmins. Wherever the Brahmins went, they naturally sought to perpetuate their own social ascendancy by inculcating their own superiority as custodians of a divine revelation and expounders of sacred laws, by surrounding their own vocation with the halo of divine inspiration and sanction. They placed themselves above king and nobility. The priest who consecrated the king presented him to the people, saying: "Here is *your* king, O people; the king of the Brahmins is Soma." Though the Brahmin did not ostensibly participate in the secular government, the king was bound to employ a Brahmin as *purohita* or house-priest, who occupied as such the position of prime-minister. In the *Aitareya Brahmanam* it is declared: "Verily the gods do not eat the food offered by the king who is without a *purohita*: Wherefore let the king, who wishes to sacrifice, place a Brahmin at the head." The king had to propitiate each one of the five destructive powers of the *purohita* to obtain *swarga*. The ways of propitiation were by servile speech, by washing his feet, by adorning him, by satiating his belly, and finally by welcoming him to the seraglio in order that he might quench the "burning, blazing fire of his *upastha*." We see all these in the customs obtaining even now in the royal household of Travancore, where the kings have Nair mothers and Nambudri Brahmin fathers.

It might seem rather strange that the kings and the nobility should have yielded the first place to the Brahmins. Elsewhere the fighting men have taken precedence and even been the spiritual guides of the people. It was the blood-bond that gave the old English society its military and social form. Something akin, represented by the word *varna*, the Vedic word for social status, was the basis of the early Hindu social system. This was superseded afterwards by the idea of ritualistic purity, but this change did not take place without a struggle. The sacred books have preserved souvenirs of the attempts made by the Kshatriyas, the nobility, to put down the power of the Brahmins. Though the Brahmins were generally the priests, we find the exceptional cases of the *rajanya* Visvamitra and Devapi who acted as priests. The former is said to have attained the status of a Brahmin by the power of austerities (*tapas*), but this position was not given him without question. "The deep-seated antagonism between the Vasistha and Visvamitra septs," says Fick, "was in reality an expression of the struggle for supermacy between the nobility and priesthood." If we may accept the legend of Parasurama as containing some historical germs, bloody wars must have characterised the rivalry for power between the Brahmins and the Kshatriyas. A country where people are divided into classes on a religious basis, the priest always succeeds in inciting at his wish one class against another. Hence the fights between the Brahmins and the Kshatriyas were in all probability fought for the former by the great mass of the people. Though the cause of these fights is said to be the robbing by the warriors of the treasures which the priests had acquired by the performance of sacrinces, yet they were essentially due to the endeavour of the warrior class to put down priestly arrogance. The rivalry between the Brahmins and the Kshatriyas could end only in the downfall of the one or the other. The nobility failed. The natural result was the theory that the Brahmin could exist without the Kshatriya, but that the Kshatriya could not exist without the Brahmin *purohita*. The Hindu theory of kingship is that the king is an absolute and responsible ruler who unites in his own person all legislature for the purpose of enforcing the rules of the various castes. No wonder that the Brahmins enjoyed many political privileges. They were exempt from taxation under all circumstances, "even if the king should starve"; for even the worst crimes they could not be executed or chastised, nor could their property be confiscated. It is not improbable that the high claims of the Brahmins to priority in the state proceeds from the *purohitas* rather than from the ordinary sacrificial priests.

The belief in the power of magic was the fertile source, not only of the abnormal development of the sacerdotal system, but also of asceticism. Of all sacrifices the greatest is that in which a human being is offered to the gods. There can be no doubt that human sacrifices were once common in India. "Despite protestant legends, despite formal disclaimers," says Prof. E. W. Hopkins, "human sacrifices existed long after the period of the Rig Veda, where it is alluded to." The *Mahavastu* says that it is the advent of the Buddha that put an end to *asvamedham*, *purushamedham*, *pundarikam* and other kinds of abominable sacrifices in India. A human sacrifice was very expensive, for ordinarily it cost one thousand cattle to buy a human victim for sacrifice. It was indeed meritorious for one to put oneself to this expense, but it would be more meritorious for the very individual to whose benefit accrued the sacrifice to immolate himself. Thus was evolved the theory and practice of self-mortification as a means of coercing the gods to bestow gifts on man. The Hindu books are full of legendary accounts of the wonderful powers attained through self-mortification and austere penance. By self-mortification Ravana became invulnerable against gods and demons. By austere fervour Nahusha obtained undisputed sway of the three worlds. By intense austerities Kshatriya Visvamitra raised himself to the Brahmin caste. In order to attain the status of a Brahmin Matanga, a chandala, went through such a course of austerities as alarmed the gods. Though his request was not granted, yet he secured the right to be honoured. Such was the profound faith of the people of Ancient India in the power of asceticism. So the *sannyasin* or the forest-haunting ascetic became the final stage in the Brahminic ideal, the aim being to seek hidden knowledge in the retirement from the world. These forest-haunting philosophers developed a new class of literature called the *Aranyakas*, in which are found the Upanishads.

The Upanishads are books containing theosophic speculations based on the Vedas. They are the source of all orthodox religious movements in Hinduism, even at the present day. In them the teachers of the highest knowledge are not Brahmins. While the Brahmins were heaping sacrifice on sacrifice and multiplying sophistical and symbolical explanations of the sacrifice, the Kshatriyas seem to have devoted their attention to the solution of the problems of life, to the understanding of the relation of the individual to the whole. In the Upanishads the Brahmins are frequently represented as going to the great Kshatriya kings to become their pupils. In the second book of the *Brihadaranyaka Upanishad* is found the following story, of which a slightly different version occurs in the *Kausitaki Upanishad* also. A proud and learned Brahmin, Balaki Gargya, comes on his journey to Ajatasatru, king of Kasi, and says to him: "I will declare to you the Brahman." The king, highly pleased, promises him a big reward of a thousand cows. The Brahmin begins to expound his wisdom: "The spirit in the sun I venerate as the Brahman." But the king interrupts him, saying that he knew that already. Then the Brahmin speaks about the spirit in the moon, in lightning, wind, fire, water, *akas*, but the king already knows all that. And whatsoever the Brahmin might say was already known to the king. The Brahmin becomes silent. But Ajatasatru asks him: "Is that all?" and the Brahmin answers: "Yes, that is all." Then the king says: "Your little knowledge is not the Brahman." Then the Brahmin desires the king to take him as a pupil;

Ajatasatru replies: "It is against nature that a Brahmin should learn from a *rajanya* and depend upon him for the understanding of the Brahman, but I shall show it to you nevertheless." In another story, found in the fifth book of the *Chandogya Upanishad* as well as in the sixth book of the *Brihadaranyaka Upanishad*, a young Brahmin, Svetaketu, comes to a convention of king Pravahana Jaivali of the Panchala country. The king puts the Brahmin youth some questions and the young Brahmin confesses his inability to answer them with the instruction given by his father. Discouraged he returns to his father and reproaches him for instructing him so poorly as to be unable to answer even one of the three questions put to him by a simple *rajanya*. The father replies: "You have known me sufficiently to understand that I taught you all I know. Come, let us go to the king and learn from him." The king received Svetaketu's father with great respect and asked him to choose a gift. The Brahmin, refusing all other gifts, chose as his gift the answers to the questions the king put to his son. At first the king was unwilling but after a while he agreed, saying: "Would that neither you nor your ancestors had trespassed on us that this truth might never have set up residence among the Brahmins. But to you, since you are so inquiring, I shall communicate our wisdom." In a third story which occurs in the fifth book of the *Chandogya Upanishad* a number of highly learned Brahmins led by Uddalaka Aruni, an inquirer after the Brahman, seek the help of Asvapathi, the king of the Kaikeya country, for disclosing to them the true nature of the "omnipresent self". The chief import of these stories, whether they be historical or legendary, is that their occurrence in genuine Brahminical books shows that the Brahmins did not claim as the inheritance of their caste the Brahman-Atman doctrine of the Upanishads. Even in philosophical discussions where a Brahmin, such as Yagnavalkya appears as the teacher, it is a Kshatriya, such as Janaka, the king of Mithila, that plays the prominent part, and the Brahmin is endeavouring to please the king by an allegorical interpretation of the sacrificial rites in the light of the Kshatriya philosophy.

Not only for the doctrine of identity of the individual soul with the world-soul does India appear to be indebted to the Kshatriya caste, but to it also seems due the theory of transmigration of souls. The Rig Veda contains no trace of belief in the transmigration of souls after death. The view that rules in its hymns is that the souls of the good go after death to Yama's heaven of light, where they lead a blissful life in the company of *pitris*, that the evil ones remain shut out from it and go into 'the nether darkness', and that there is no return of either to earth life. In the Brahmanams there is the added doctrine that man is liable to retribution for his good or evil deeds, that he will expiate actions done in this world by repeated births and rebirths in the other world. In the Upanishads the retribution for good or evil deeds is not confined to repeated rebirths of the soul in the other world, but the soul has to come again on earth to work out the reward or penalty which good or evil deeds necessitate. This is the doctrine of transmigration of souls as it now obtains in India. Of this doctrine of metempsychosis king Pravahana tells the Brahmin Goutama: "This knowledge has not till now resided with a Brahmin." This doctrine of reincarnation appears to have been a hereditary secret teaching of the Rajanyas. One of the aspects of animism is that conception is the reincarnation of a human or animal soul. The thoughtful Kshatriya modified this doctrine with a view to reconcile the apparent conflict between his ideal of justice and the stern realities of life wherein not infrequently the wicked enjoy and the righteous suffer. He must have seen many unrighteous individuals in the Brahmin caste and many righteous individuals in the other castes. Naturally he tried to console himself by reflection. If the aim of life was the freeing of the soul from rebirths in abodes of punishment or from rebirths on earth in the body of a man of lower caste or in a degrading animal existence, why should it not be possible for one's soul by obedience to the will of the gods, veneration of the Brahmins, performance of religious duties, and observance of the laws and ordinances of one's own caste, not only to gain rewards in heaven, but also to be reborn on earth in the family of a higher caste, even as a Brahmin?

The continuance of the sacrificial system indicates that the Brahmins were not eager to accept the progressive ideas of the Kshatriyas. But when these ideas got into the air and became popular, the Brahmins could not help adopting them and endeavour to harmonise them with their practices By representing ritual and sacrifice as the first step to knowledge, they combined two wholly incongruous elements.

They even turned the theory of metempsychosis to their own benefit. The individual soul could ascend to the status of a Brahmin only after passing through a series of births. Consequently, the being that attained this position deserved reverence from all. Only as a Brahmin who had undergone the preparatory training could the individual soul attain the supreme knowledge of the oneness of the individual atman with the Brahman or the universal atman. Although the Kshatriya teachers of the Upanishads perceived the hollowness of the sacrificial system and its absurd symbolic character, they did not, beyond consoling themselves with the thought that he who knew the highest Brahman became himself Brahman and therefore immortal, openly proclaim their knowledge to the people at large and pose as teachers in opposition to the priestly class. They taught their doctrines only to some Brahmins who as a matter of course kept their knowledge secret. Even in open discussions this teaching was not imparted in the hearing of all. In the fourth book of the *Brihadaranyaka* Upanishad we have an account of a public disputation on the knowledge that liberates the soul between the Rishi Yagnavalkya and the Brahmins present at a sacrifice by Janaka, the king of Videha. Artabhaga the Jaratkarava questions Yajnavalkya as to what happens to a man who has not won liberation when he dies. Yajnavalkya says: "Give me thy hand, good Artabhaga; we will find out the answer to thy question, but this is no matter to discuss in public." So they go out and confer together and come to the conclusion that the law of Karma sends the soul from body to body and that a man therefore becomes holy by holy works and unholy by unholy works in previous lives. The teachers of the Upanishads never attempted to bring their teachings into contact with the daily life of the ordinary man.

It is a glory of Buddhism that it diffused broad-cast what was hidden in the community of the learned. Like the teachers of the Upanishads the founder of Buddhism, Goutama Sakyamuni, was a Kshatriya. He thoroughly grasped the teachings of the Upanishads and developed them to their logical consequences and promulgated the *saddharma* (true principles) in opposition to the *sanatana dharma*, the "eternal principles" of the Brahmins and their compromising Kshatrya followers. The pouring of the new wine of truth into the old bottles of superstition cannot but give new vitality to error and prolong its duration and bring about worse enervation. Hypocrisy may be a valuable social virtue, but all progress is due to loyalty to one's own intelligence and fidelity to truth. Gautama Sakyamuni saw the futility of atoning for evil deeds by the destruction of life and the impossibility of practising religion without compassion and *noblesse oblige*. He therefore strenuously opposed the sacrificial system. The sacrificial rites and their attendant superstitions and the knowledge by which the Brahmins pretended to put men in relation with the gods appeared to him a mere delusion. He spoke of the Brahmins as blind leaders of the blind. If, as the Upanishads taught, the Brahman pervaded all things and was identical with the individual soul, where was the spiritual inequality between man and man? He therefore rejected the caste system as a harmful institution. He taught that salvation from sorrow and suffering was within the reach of every one, whether he be a Brahmin, a Kshatriya, a Vaisya, a Sudra, or a Mlecha, that every one, whatever may be his birth or rank, could attain the goal by the attainment of true knowledge and by devotion to the welfare of fellow beings. He carried the theory of reincarnation to its utmost spiritual extent, and proclaimed that the actions of men are the sole controlling influence on their past, present and future. He was thus led to deny the existence of any external being or god who could interfere with the immutable law of cause and effect. He attempted to link together all mankind as parts of one universal whole and therefore denounced the isolated self-seeking of the human heart as "the heresy of individuality." By basing his teachings on the liberation of the individual from suffering he endeavoured to make men moral, compassionate and benevolent. The Buddha demonstrated the futility of caste distinctions by the following simple arguments.

"Between ashes and gold there is a marked difference, but between a Brahmana and a Chandala there is nothing of the kind. A Brahmana is not produced like fire by the friction of dry wood; he does not descend from the sky nor from the air, nor does he come out piercing the earth. The Brahmana is brought forth from the womb of a woman in exactly the same way as a Chandala. All human beings have organs exactly alike; there is not the slightest difference in kind. In plants, insects, fishes, snakes, birds, quadrupeds the marks that constitute the species are abundant, whereas amongst men this is not the case. Neither the hair, nor the formation of the skull, nor the colour of the skin, nor the vocal organ, nor any other part of the body exhibits any specific differences. Further, when sexual intercourse takes place between the members of different castes, the children in all cases take after the mother as well as the father, and there is no difficulty in assigning them to their proper parents. What then is the support for supposing the existence of different species among mankind?

"The Brahmana is a specifically Indian phenomenon. In the neighbouring countries no Brahmana exists. In those countries there are only masters and slaves. Those who are rich are masters, and those who are poor are slaves. The rich may become poor, and the poor rich. Even in India when a Kshatriya, a Vaisya, or a Sudra abounds in wealth, the members of the Brahmana caste serve him, they wait for his commands, and use soft words to gratify him; to minister to his wants they wake up before him and do not go to sleep till he has retired to rest. Where then lies the difference between the four castes? The declaration of the Brahmanas that they alone are the highest caste and others are of low caste is an empty sound.

"If a Brahmana commits sin, he suffers for it like every other man. Like every other man the Brahmana also has to abstain from evil deeds, if he desires salvation. The ethical world-order gives the lie to the theory of the specific inequalities among mankind. The native capacities and talents are of the same kind everywhere. The Sudra who is despised for his caste is as much capable of good thoughts and noble deeds as the Brahmana. If a bath can purify a Brahmana, it can equally purify a man of any other caste. Nor does fire show any special regard for differences of caste. The fire, produced by the members of the so-called highest caste by rubbing costly fragrant sticks, arises just in the same way as that produced by the members of the so-called lowest caste by rubbing pieces of wood from a dirty foul-smelling dog-trough, or swine-trough? On the contrary the good sense of the Brahmanas themselves proves that it is the ethical worth of an individual that confers superiority. For, in distributing alms they prefer an ethically good natured man, even when he may exhibit no distinguishing marks, nay, even when he may not have gone through the initiatory ceremony known as "second birth". It follows therefore that, while exact information can be obtained as to the purity or impurity of an individual's conduct, no exact information can be obtained as regards birth and descent.

"By birth and descent all men are alike; they become different only through differences in occupation, and they are designated accordingly. Some are called husband men, some artisans, some merchants, some kings, some robbers, some priests, and so on. In one and the same caste different members follow different professions. Have we not among the Brahmanas physicians; necromancers; musicians; merchants; agriculturists owning cattle, poultry and slaves; wealthy landholders who give much wealth as the portion of their daughters and receive much when their sons are married; butchers who kill animals and sell their flesh; those that provide gratification for the lust of others; those who tell lucky hours; those who sit *dharāna* and enforce gifts from kings; those that live like savages in the wilderness; those who get their livelihood after the manner of those who break into houses to steal; beggars with long hair, dirty teeth, immense nails, filthy bodies, and heads covered with dust and lice; those who profess to be released from all desires and to be ready to release others also? How, then, can it be said that Brahma made the Brahmana for the performance of sacrifices and the study of the Veda, the Kshatriya for sovereignty and command, the Vaisya for ploughing the land, and the Sudra for serving and obeying the rest? If we look closely, we see no difference between the body of a prince and that of a slave. What is essential is that which may dwell in the most miserable frame, and which the wisest have always saluted and honoured. The talk of "high and low castes," of "pure Brahmanas, the only sons of Brahma", is nothing but cant. The four castes are equal. He is a Chandala who cherishes hatred; who torments and kills living beings; who steals, or commits adultery; who does not pay his debts; who maltreats aged parents; or fails to support them; who gives evil counsel and hides the truth; who does not return hospitality nor render it; who exalts himself and debases others; who ignores the virtues of others and is jealous of their success. He is a Brahmana who is free from sin. Not by birth does one become a Chandala, nor by birth does one become a Brahmana; by deeds one becomes a Chandala, by deeds one becomes a Brahmana."

Just as the light of the sun and moon shines upon all the world, on the virtuous and the wicked, on the foul-smelling and the fragrant, on the high and the low, just as their beams are sent down equally, without partiality, so did the teaching of the Buddha diffuse its intellectual and ethical light on all without any difference. All were admitted without distinction of caste and creed into the Sangha. All the ordained disciples of the Buddha gave up caste when they joined the order. But this renunciation of caste does not appear to have been demanded of his lay followers. Perhaps the social conditions prevalent during his time prevented Sakyamuni from preaching a general crusade against caste. But the caste distinctions that obtained among the Buddhist laity had no religious significance. An incident in the life of Emperor Asoka brings out clearly the bearing of caste in Indian Buddhist society. After Asoka became a Buddhist, it was his custom whenever he met the ordained disciples of the Buddha to salute them by touching their feet with his head. On one occasion his Hindu Minister told him: "My lord, it is not seemly for thee thus to prostrate thyself before the *bhikshus* of all castes." To this the Emperor replied: "Yea, by a sentiment of pride and delusion, fostered by beauty and power, dost thou desire to dissuade me from prostrating myself at the feet of the religieux. And if my head, that worthless object which no man desires even when he may obtain it for nothing, meet an occassion for purification and acquire some merit thereby, what is there unlawful in that? In the Sakya-bhikshus thou regardest nought save the renunciation of caste and thou beholdest not their virtues; wherefore, puffed with pride of birth, thou forgettest thy error, both thyself and others. Caste may be considered when it is a question of marriage or of an invitation, but not of the Dharma; for the Dharma is concerned with virtues, and virtues have nothing to do with caste. When a man of high birth falls into vice, he is blamed by the world; wherefore when a man of low caste is virtuous, should he not inspire respect? It is by reason of their character that men's bodies are honoured or despised. The Sakya-bhikshus should be revered, as their character has been completely changed and purified by the words of the Compassionate One."

That the caste distinctions observed by the Buddhist laity had no religious significance is also proved by the fact that the Buddhists never assigned a supernatural or mystic origin to differences of caste. According to the Buddhists mankind had in the beginning all property in common. Later a distribution took place and each person laid up provisions for oneself. After this it happenned that one person took another's property without the consent of the latter, as if it were his own. The latter punished the evil-doer by his own hand. Then in view of what was happening, people thought: "Let us assemble together and choose from our midst those who are the finest looking, the largest, the strongest, and let us make them lords over our fields and they shall punish those of us who do what is punishable, and they shall recompense those of us who do what is praiseworthy, and from the products of the fields and of the fruits we gather we shall give them a portion." So they gathered together and chose a suitable person to be lord over their fields. As he was lord over the fields and kept them from harm, he was called Kshatriya or "protector of the fields." Some persons, to find happiness in meditation and seclusion, left their villages for the wilds. These were called "detached minds" or Brahmanas. Later, some of these gave up contemplation, composed *mantras* forming the Vedas; from their habit of repeating them they were called *pathakas*. Among those that lived in villages some applied themselves to different handicrafts and occupations in their homes, made different kinds of things and offered them for sale. These were called Vaisyas or merchants. Thus originated according to the early Buddhists the several castes in a natural way and not as the Brahmins claimed in a transcendental manner. For the Brahmins there is caste among the gods and also animals and even in the metres of their holy verses. For the Brahmins the countries where the system of castes does not exist are *mlechcha* and those that dislike the system of castes are the enemies of their religion.

Though the Brahmins saw that the teaching of Sakyamuni was subversive of the system of caste and of the supremacy of the born priest, yet they did not experience its full practical significance till Saddharna came under the aegis of a sovereign power. Though in his day Sakyamuni was patronised by many kings, the Sangha, constituted on a democratic basis, was concerned only with the spiritual uplifting of its members and those that patronised it. Buddhism took no part in any struggle for temporal power. On the other hand, according to Brahminic theories, the king ruled only through the divine power of the *purohita*, whose will could override that of the king. Though the Brahmins consecrated the king of the people, yet he was not their king. Soma was the sovereign of the Brahmins. Hence Brahminism could not compromise itself with any temporal power striving to be independent of the spiritual power of the Brahmin. Things went on smoothly till indigenous kings ruled over India. There is no indication that before the time of Asoka the teaching of the Buddha was known beyond very narrow limits. Alexander's invasion of India introduced foreigners into the land. He left behind him colonists and a few satrapies. On Alexander's death his Indian dominions fell into a state of disorder. The Indian king, Poros, who claimed control over the satrapy west of the Indus, was murdered by an assassin hired by Eudemos, the satrap of that province. The most powerful indigenous king who owned allegiance to the foreigner was thus removed out of the way, and the field became open to adventurers. An adventurous Maurya chief, Chandragupta, made himself master of the Panjab. A wily Brahmin, named Chanakya, slew the last king of the ruling dynasty of Magadha, then the largest and richest state in the interior, and made Chandragupta king. Chanakya being the prime-minister, Brahminism exercised its sway on the destiny of empire in India.

The Maurya empire, founded by Chandragupta, passed in 272 B.C. to his grandson Asoka Vardhana, one of the most illustrious monarchs of India. A record of his work is preserved in the Edicts which he caused to be engraved on rocks and stone-pillars. His rule extended all over Northern India from sea to sea and as far south as Pulicat. In 216 B.C., he undertook a campaign against Kalinga, in which "one hundred and fifty thousand were carried away captive, one hundred thousand were slain and many times that number perished." One of his Edicts says; "His Majesty feels remorse on account of the conquest of the Kalingas, because, during the subjugation of a previously unconquered country, slaughter, death, and taking away captive of the people necessarily occur, whereat His Majesty feels profound sorrow and regret." There is no reason to doubt that Asoka's conversion to Buddhism was due to his remorse for the sufferings caused by the carnage in his conquest of Kalinga. The ethics of the Edicts are purely Buddhist. The idea of duty as associated with the notions of caste is dropped. The teaching of the Edicts is purely human and severely practical. The Edicts ignore the existence of a supreme deity and insist on the necessity of man's own self-exertions to obtain happiness. The object aimed at is the happiness of all living creatures, man and beast. One Edict expressly a vows the authority of the Blessed Buddha as the foundation of Asoka's ethical system.

In the moral teaching of Asoka prominence is given to two virtues, namely respect for the sanctity of animal life and reverence to parents, superiors and elders. In the Brahminic system the slaughtering of animals for sacrifice played a dominant part. In the *Satapatha Brahmanam* it is stated that men, horses, bulls, rams, and she-goats were used for sacrifice. In the *Asvalayana Grihya Sutra* mention is made of several sacrifices in which the slaughter of cattle formed a part. The Buddha preached against this vain slaughtering of animals. Asoka therefore prohibited all bloody sacrifices and all vain killing of animals. Many kinds of animals were absolutely protected from slaughter in any circumstances; on fifty days in the year killing under any pretext was categorically forbidden. Many restrictions were imposed on the slaying of animals for food. In his first Rock Edict Asoka promulgated: "Here (in the capital) no animal may be slaughtered for sacrifice, nor may the holiday feast be held, because His Sacred and Gracious Majesty the King sees much offence in the holiday feast, although in certain places holiday feasts are excellent in the sight of His Sacred and Gracious Majesty the King. Formerly, in the kitchen of His Sacred and Gracious Majesty the King, each day many hundred thousands of living creatures were slaughtered to curries. But now, when this pious Edict is being written, only three living creatures are slaughtered (daily) for curry, to wit, two peacocks and one antelope—the antelope, however, not invariably. Even those three living creatures shall not henceforth be slaughtered." Another feature of the Brahminical system is the importance attached to ritual. Rites and ceremonies were considered by the Brahmins as essential for man's well-being. The Buddha declared the belief in the efficacy of purificatory ceremonies and rites (*silavrata paramarsa*) as an obstacle to progress (*samyojana*) and their incapability to afford emanicipation from misery. Hence in his ninth Rock Edict Asoka promulgated the nature of true ceremonial: "Thus saith His Sacred and

Gracious Majesty the King:—People perform ceremonies on occasions of sickness, the weddings of sons, the weddings of daughters, the birth of children, and departure on journeys. On these and other similar occasions people perform ceremonies (auspicious rites). But at such times the womankind perform many manifold, trivial, and worthless ceremonies (*mangalams*). Ceremonies have certainly to be performed, although that sort bears little fruit. This sort, however,—the ceremonial of Dharma—bears great fruit. In it are included proper treatment of slaves, honour to teachers, gentleness towards living creatures, and liberality towards Sramanas and Brahmanas (those free from sin). These things and others of the same kind are called the ceremonial of Dharma. Therefore ought a father, son, brother, master, friend, or comrade, nay, even a neighbour, to say: 'This is meritorious, this is the ceremonial to be performed until the attainment of the desired end.' And it has been said—'Alms giving is meritorious.' But there is no such gift or favour as the gift of Dharma, the favour of Dharma. Therefore should a friend, lover, relative, or comrade advise on such and such an occasion, 'this is to be done, this is meritorious, by this it is possible for you to gain heaven (happiness)'. And what is better worth doing than that by which heaven is gained?"

No sovereign ever rendered to his country a greater service than did Asoka to his country. "The care taken to publish the imperial edicts and commemorative records by incising them in imperishable characters, most skilfully executed, on rocks and pillars situated in great cities, on main lines of communication, or at sacred spots frequented by pilgrims, implies that a knowledge of reading and writing was widely diffused, and that many people must have been able to read the documents. The same inference may be drawn from the fact that the inscriptions are composed, not in any learned scholastic tongue, but in vernacular dialects intelligible to the common people, and modified when necessary to suit local needs. It is probable that learning was fostered by the numerous monasteries and that the boys and girls in hundreds of villages learned their lessons from the monks and nuns, as they do now in Burma from the monks. Asoka, it should be noted, encouraged nunneries, and makes particular reference more than once to female lay disciples as well as to nuns. I think it likely that the percentage of literacy among the Buddhist population in Asoka's time was higher than it is now in many provinces of British India. The latest returns show that in the United Provinces of Agra and Oudh, which include many great cities and ancient capitals, the number of persons per 1000 able to read and write amounts to only 57 males and 2 females. In Burma where the Buddhist monasteries flourish, the corresponding figures are 378 and 45. I believe that the Buddhist monasteries and nunneries in the days of their glory must have been, on the whole, powerful agencies for good in India, and that the disappearance of Buddhism was a great loss to the country." (V. Smith)

Asoka possessed in abundance what Aristotle calls practical wisdom, the gift and ability of the statesman to guide the organization, habitation and education of mankind in the direction of theoretical wisdom, that higher activity which finds its expression in high thinking, fine art and religion. His aim was the creation of a kingdom, of righteousness without a god, the government playing the part of providence in guiding the people in the rightway. No wonder that he is venerated as *Dharmarajah* (king of Dharma) from the Volga to Japan and from Siam to Lake Baikal. But astonishing is the fact that his name finds no mention in Brahminical literature. The reason of this designed omission is obvious. Though Asoka did not attempt to put down Brahminism, yet he endeavoured to govern his empire without Brahminic aid, which, according to Brahminic theories, is quite improper. Says the *Satapatha Brahmanam*: "It is quite improper that a king should be without a Brahmin, for, whatever deed he does, unsped by the priesthood, therein he succeeds not. Wherefore a Kshatriya who intends to do a deed ought by all means to resort to a Brahmin, for he verily succeeds in the deed sped by the Brahmin." Asoka openly avowed his preference for Buddhism and prohibited bloody sacrifices, which were so essential to the Brahminic religion. While his Hindu grandfather prohibited the slaughter of cows, Asoka rendered no special protection to cows or other horned cattle. One of the most striking features of Brahminic legislation was the reduction of punishment in consideration of the caste of the criminal. Brahmins were not subject to corporal punishment; they were allowed special indulgences in almost every case As a rule Brahmins were exempt from capital punishment, except in the case of high treason when a Brahmin might be executed by drowning, while a member of any other caste should be burnt alive. Brahmins were exempt from liability to judicial torture for the purpose of extracting a confession. Asoka undid all this. He introduced a stringent code of regulations applicable to all cases of the population throughout his empire without distinction of class or creed. He insisted upon all his officers strictly observing the principle *danda samata* and *vyavahara samata*, that is, the equality of all in the eye of the law, irrespective of caste, colour and creed. An official machinery was provided for the strict enforcement of his orders and for the promulgation of Saddharma. In his third Rock Edict Asoka says: "Everywhere in my dominions the subordinate officials and the commissioner and the district officer must proceed every five years on circuit, as well for their other business as for this special purpose, namely, to give instruction in the Dharma." A special agency of censors was employed for the purpose of carrying out the regulations relating to Saddharma. In the fifth Rock Edict we read: "Now in all the long time past, officers known as censors of Dharma (*dharma mahamatyas*) never had existed, whereas such censors were created by me." The fruit of all this exertion on behalf of Saddharma was, as recorded in the Rupnath Minor Rock Edict, that those who were regarded as veritable gods (*bhu-deva*) in Jambudvipa were shown to be false, a statement which should be understood as indicating that the immemorial privileged position of the Brahmins was seriously affected by the zealous efforts of Asoka in propagating Buddhism.

Even in the time of Asoka the Brahmin priesthood must have been covertly exerting themselves to bring about his downfall, but his official machinery was too strong for them. As soon as the sceptre dropped from his strong hand, the influence of the Brahmin re-asserted itself. The glory of the Maurya dynasty gradually waned, until the last king of the line was treacherously assassinated by his commander-in-chief, Pushyamitra (185 B.C.). As a patron of the Brahmins he proscribed Buddhism. He "indulged in a savage persecution of Buddhism, burning monasteries and slaying monks (*bhikshus*) from Magadha to Jalandhar, in the Panjab." He revived the bloody sacrifices believed by the Brahmins to possess the highest saving efficacy. He proclaimed himself a paramount sovereign, and having been consecrated by the Brahmins for the *rajasuya* sacrifice, he let loose a horse to wander into foreign territory. The horse wandering on the bank of the Sindhu fell into the hands of the Yavanas, but was saved by the party following it. So he celebrated with great pomp the ancient rite of the horse-sacrifice (*asvamedha*). In this period of Brahminical reaction appeared probably the famous law book of Manu, in which the most supercilious claims were set up for the Brahmins and the caste system was carried to an absurd extent. Various passages in the Code of Manu indicate how little the claim of the Brahmins to divinity suffered through the organised Buddhist propaganda of Asoka. "The Brahmins are to be venerated at all times, as they are the highest divinity." "By his very origin the Brahmin is a god, even to the gods." "Although Brahmins employ themselves in all sorts of mean occupation, they must invariably be honoured; for they are something transcendently divine." The interests of the Brahmins are specially advanced in the Code. "Whatever exists in the universe, is all in effect the wealth of the Brahmin, since the Brahmin is entitled to it all by his primogeniture and eminence of birth." The Code deprives the Sudra of all rights. "The Sudra shall not acquire wealth even if he be in a position to do so, as such conduct gives offence to the Brahmin." "A Brahmin may seize without hesitation, if he be distressed for a subsistence, the goods of his Sudra slave; for, as that slave can have no property, his master may take his goods" "A man of the servile class, whether bought or unbought, the Brahmin may compel to perform servile duty, because such a man was created by the Self-existent for the purpose of serving Brahmins. A Sudra, though emanicipated by his master, is not released from a state of servitude; for, from a state which is natural to him, by whom can he be divested?" "Whatever crime a Brahmin might commit, his person and property were not to be injured; but whoever struck a Brahmin with a blade of grass would become an inferior quadruped during twenty one transmigrations." Of the three twice-born castes Brahmins were absolutely prohibited from marrying Sudra women. Any defilement by such an alliance was declared to be beyond all expiation. The men of the twice-born castes were ordered to choose their first wives from their own class, and a Sudra must not marry into a higher caste. Though there was apparently no absolute bar to intermarriage between the different *varnas* with the above-mentioned exceptions, marriage with a Sudra woman by any twice-born man was regarded as a debasement of the purity of the family stock. But all these were harmless in comparison with the new principles introduced into the Code for the purpose of reducing to miserable life numberless human beings who had done no wrong except that their origin did not agree with the religio-political scheme of the Brahmins. Good seed in a bad soil gives of course poorer return than in good soil; still the crop is endurable But weed introduced into good soil produces weed abundantly. Similarly the children were below the father if he married a wife of a higher caste. This theory gave birth to a great number of mixed castes, who were more or less despised. The lowest and most execrable caste was that of the Chandala, the offspring of a Sudra father and a Brahmin mother. The Chandala had to live far from the abodes of other men and carry signs by which he might be recognised and his polluting contact avoided. He should possess only common animals like dogs and donkeys, eat out of broken vessels, put on the dresses of the dead, etc. But the Chandala was not the last in the Brahminic scale; his offspring, though his wife had belonged only to the Sudra caste, was necessarily still below him. Thus originated a great number of mixed castes, one more despised than the other and one despising another, the progenitors of the depressed castes of the present day whose untouchability is a very characteristic feature of the caste system.

To this period must be assigned the second stage of development of the *Mahabharata*. According to Prof. E W. Hopkins, "the Pandu epic, as we have it, represents a period not only subsequent to Buddhism, 500 B C., but also to the Greek invasion, 300 B C. Buddhistic supremacy already decadent is implied by the passages which allude contemptuously to the Buddhist monuments as having ousted the temples of the gods...... The present epic, if it records anything historical, records the growth of a great power in Hindustan, a power that could not have arisen before Buddhistic supremacy without leaving a trace of the mighty name of Pandu in the early literature. There is no such trace; moreover, even the idea of any such power as our epic depicts was unknown before the great empire that arose under Buddhism." This view is supported by the mention not only of Buddhist relic mounds but also of Yavanas as the allies of Kurus. It is not improbable that king Dattamitra described in the epic as taking a direct part in the war is identical with the Bactrian king Demetrius (180—165 B.C.) and that Bhagadatta, who is described as the king of Yavanas ruling over Naraka in the west and as an old friend of the father of Yudhistira, is identical with the Bactrian king Apollodotus (160 B.C). All scholars seem to agree in the view that the *Mahabharata* has passed through at least three stages of development. In the beginning there were only old songs about the ancient feud, referred to in the Vedas, between the two neighbouring tribes of the Kurus and Panchalas and the heroes who played a part in it, and these were handed down by word of mouth and recited in popular assemblies or at great public sacrifices. These disconnected battle songs were firstly worked up by some poetic genius into a comparatively short epic (of about eight thousand verses), describing the tragic fate of the Kuru race, who, with justice and virtue on their side, perished through the treachery of the victorious sons of Pandu. The second development of the epic took place in connection with the *rajasuya* sacrifice of Pushyamitra. The victorious Pandus were represented in a favourable light, the bloody sacrifices of the Brahmins were praised and the observance of caste rules was reestablished. In the first stage appeared only the figure of Brahma as the highest god, but in the second stage two other great gods, Siva and especially Vishnu, made their appearance. The Brahmins had not much reverence for the gods whom they could coerce by their *mantras* and by the magic of their sacrifices, and put themselves on a level of equality with the gods as their terrestrial representatives. Yet they needed some deities with human traits to serve as a set-off against the Buddha who was venerated almost as a god. They found two such deities in Agni and Vishnu. These two deities were directly connected with the sacrifice. "Agni is the lower half and Vishnu is the upper half of the sacrifice." Vishnu forsooth is the sacrifice; by his strides he obtained for the gods that all pervading power which now belongs to them." "This whole Agni has now been completed: he now is the deity Rudra. Upon him the gods bestowed the highest form, immortality. Flaming he there stood longing for food. The gods were afraid of him, lest he should hurt them." In the *Mahabharata* the fire god is identified with Rudra. The production of fire from the firesticks and the apparent similarity of the process to sexual reproduction led to the worship of this god under the symbol of the power of propagation, the *lingam*. In the *Mahabharata* we are told that it is the organ of generation which is worshipped under the name of Mahadeva. The Brahmins thus raised the sacrifice to the status of a god, sometimes in the form of Vishnu and sometimes in the form of Siva the euphemistic name of Agni, but always with the express purpose of exalting themselves. The mother Earth is questioned as to what cleanses the sins of a man leading the domestic mode of life. Mother Earth's plain answer is: "One should serve the Brahmins. A Brahmin by birth alone becomes an object of adoration with all creatures." In another place a Chandala performing austere penance is told that "this object of thy desire, the status of a Brahmin, which is the foremost of everything, is incapable of being won by penance." The *Mahabharata* declares: "From the order of brute life one attains to the status of humanity. If born as a human being, he is sure to take birth as a Pukkasa or a Chandala. One having taken birth in that sinful order of existence one has to wander in it for a very long time. Passing a period of one thousand years in that order, one attains next to the status of a Sudra. In the Sudra order one has to wander thirty thousand years before one acquires the status of a Vaisya. After wandering for a time that is sixty times longer than what has been stated as the period of the Sudra existence, one attains to the Kshatriya order. After wandering for a time that is measured by multiplying the period last named by two hundred, one becomes born in the race of such a Brahmin as lives by the profession of arms. After a time measured by multiplying the period last named by three hundred, one takes birth in the race of a Brahmin that is given to the recitation of the *gayātri* and other *mantras*. After a time measured by multiplying the last named period by four hundred, one takes birth in the race of such a Brahmin as is conversant with the Vedas and the scriptures." Only the Brahmin as such, by subjugating joy and grief, desire and aversion, vanity and evil speech, can attain salvation. So no one can attain salvation without being first born in "the race of such a Brahmin as is conversant with the Vedas and the scriptures." Thus the observance of the rules of caste was enforced on the basis of the theory of transmigration of souls.

The dynasty of Pushyamitra came to an end with the death of its last king, contrived by his Brahmin minister, Vasudeva. Vasudeva founded the Kanva dynasty. The last of the Kanvas was slain about 28 B.C. by one of the Andhra kings of Satavahana family, who had their capital at Srikakulam on the lower course of the Krishna. Officially the Andhra kings were Brahminical Hindus, but they were not inimical to the Buddhists. One of them, Gautamiputra Sri Satakarni, posed as the champion of both Brahminical Hinduism and Buddhism as against the creeds of the casteless foreigners, Sakas, Pallavas, and prided himself as being the defender of caste rules In the early decades of the first century after Christ, a tribe of Turki nomads, called Yueh-chi, occupied the Bactrian lands south of the Oxus and settled down into a territorial nation, and in due time the chief of one of their sections, known as Kadphises I, succeeded in becoming the soul monarch of the Yueh-chi nation. After consolidating his power in Bactria he suppressed the Indo-Greek and Indo-Parthian principalities to the west of the Indus and extended his empire from the frontiers of Persia to the Indus. He was succeeded by his son, Kadphises II, who probably conquered the Panjab and a considerable part of the Gangetic plain, even as far as Benares. Kadphises II was succeeded by Kanishka in 78 A.D.; the monuments, inscriptions and coins of his time prove that his authority extended all over North-Western India, probably as far south as the Vindhyas, as well as the remote regions beyond the Pamir Pass. Penetrating far into the interior of India and overcoming the king residing at Pataliputra, he carried away with him the famous Buddhist patriarch, Asvagosha. Being a fervent Buddhist he erected a great relic tower in his capital, Purushapura (modern Peshawar), and convoked a Buddhist council at Jalandhara, which prepared a grand summary in sanskrit verse of the teachings of the Buddha.

The Yueh-chi conquests opened up the overland commercial route between India and the Roman empire and brought about a contact between Indian, Zoroastrian, Gnostic and Hellenistic religions. Either owing to an interaction between these religions, or to the desire to obtain adherents from other religious circles, or to a spontaneous natural development, Buddhism took a new shape. According to strict Buddhist teaching each man has to work out his own salvation which can in no way be helped by supernatural grace, priestly absolution, magical rites, or sacramental ceremonies; the Buddha, though wiser and greater than all the gods, is a human being. The new Buddhism developed the belief in the divinity of the Buddha, in the efficacy of faith and in saviour-bodhisats. The deification of the Buddha was the natural consequence of the elevation of Buddha to a loftier sphere than that assigned to Brahma-Sahampathi, the lord of all. The trustful reverence shown by all his disciples towards their beloved teacher was not far removed from religious adoration. In the *Milindapanha* Nagasena says that a man with a wicked nature, if he will only direct his thoughts earnestly towards Buddha, will not enter purgatory but will be reborn in heaven. Similarly the *Amitayur-dhyana Sutra* of the newer Buddhism declares that the man who with steadfast faith and quiet mind calls upon the name of Amitabha for a period of only a week, or even for a single day, may face death with perfect calmness; for Amitabha, attended by a host of celestial Bodhisats, will assuredly appear before his dying eyes and will carry him away to be reborn in buds of lotus flowers in a paradise called *Sukhavati* where, learning the good law preached to them by Amitabha, the celestial reflection of Gautama Sakyamuni, they grow happily according to their deserts and finally attain Nirvana. As morals are irksome, a religion has, in order to be popular, to proffer a substitute for morals in the form of a mechanical dispensation from all sins of commission and omission. We may therefore regard with Otto Wecker that the new Buddhism is a natural development of the old Buddhism. He says: "In strange contrast to the theoretical universality of the message of salvation, there stood from the beginning the difficulty with which the redeeming knowledge was to be gained, a difficulty so great that in fact the salvation of Buddha could never be a salvation for all, especially not for the many small and poor and weak. As soon as the consequences were drawn from the universality of the salvation which the Buddha preached, the exclusiveness of the pure doctrine must have been shattered; the postulates and ideas must necessarily be levelled and accomodated to the needs of everyday people as soon as the sermon becomes serious with its 'All ye, come unto me.' Is not this what happened? We need only point to the transformation of the Nirvana idea to illustrate by a classical example the process of conversion which changed the pure teaching of Buddha into a popular religion... A similar transformation of the person of the Buddha was the natural consequence of this evolution"

The first great exponent of this new Buddhism was Asvagosha, the versatile patriarch of the Buddhist Church in the time of Kanishka. This Buddhist genius has left a small tract called *Vajrasuchi*, which reveals to us the attitude of the later Buddhists towards the claims arrogated to themselves by the Brahmins. He tries to disprove the supercilious claims of the Brahmins from the standpoint of their own books. The argument of the *Vajrasuchi* may be summarised thus:

"Granted that the Vedas, the Smritis and the Dharmasutras, are true and valid, and that all the teachings at variance with them are invalid, still the assertion that the Brahmin is the highest of the four castes can not be maintained. What is Brahminhood? Is it the life principle *(jiva)*, or descent *(jati)*, or the body *(kaya)*, or learning *(vidya)*, or rites *(achara)*, or acts *(karma)*, or knowledge of the Vedas?

"If the life principle constituted Brahminhood, how could, as is stated in the Vedas, quadrupeds and other animals have become gods? According to the *Mahabharata* seven hunters and ten deer of the hill of Kalingala, a goose of the lake Manasasara, a Chakravaka of Sharadvipa, were born as Brahmins in Kurukshetra, and became very learned in the Vedas. In his *Dharmasastra* Manu says: "Whatever Brahmin learned in the four Vedas with their *angas* and *upangas* receives gifts or fees from a Sudra, shall for twelve births be an ass, for sixty births a hog, and seventy births a dog." Hence it is evident that it is not the life principle that constitutes Brahminhood.

"If Brahminhood depended on descent or parentage, how could this be reconciled with the statement of the Smriti that many Munis had no Brahmin mothers? Achala Muni was born of an elephant; Kesa Pingala of an owl; Suka Muni of a parrot; Kapila of a monkey; Sringa Rishi of a deer; Vyasa from a fisher woman; Kausika Muni from a female Sudra; Parasara from a Chandalini; and Vasishta from a strumpet. Visvamitra, though a Kshatriya, became the founder of a Brahmin family. Kanvayana Brahmins trace their descent from Ajamidha, a Kshatriya. The two sons of Nabhagarishta, who were Vaisyas, attained to the status of Brahmanas. If one born of a Brahmin father or mother was a Brahmin, then even the child of a slave *(dasa* or *dasi)* might become a Brahmin. If he alone was a Brahmin, whose father and mother were both Brahmins, then it must be established that the parents themselves were pure Brahmins. But the mothers of the parent race of Brahmins were not, any of them, free from the suspicion of having committed adultery with Sudras. "In human society," says Yudisthira in the *Mahabharata (vanaparva),* "it is difficult to ascertain one's caste, because of promiscuous intercourse among the four orders. Men belonging to all the orders begot (promiscuously) offspring upon women of all the orders. And of men, speech, sexual intercourse, birth and death are common. And to this the Rishis have borne testimony, by using at the beginning of a sacrifice such expressions as—'of what caste soever we may be, we celebrate the sacrifice'." Further, according to the *Manavadharmasastra* a Brahmin who ate flesh lost instantly his rank; and also he who sold wax or salt, or milk became a Sudra in three days If Brahminhood depended on birth, how could it be lost by any acts however degrading? Could an eagle by alighting on the earth be turned into a crow?

"Is the body then the Brahmin? Then fire (Agni) would become the murderer of a Brahmin, when it consumed his corpse, and such also would be every one of the relatives of a Brahmin, who might consign his body to the flames. Again, every one born of a Brahmin, though his mother was a Sudra, would be a Brahmin, being the bone of the bone and flesh of the flesh of his father. But according to the *Mahabharata* the son that is begotten by a Brahmin on a Sudra wife is called *parasava,* implying one born of a corpse, for a Sudra woman's body is as inauspicious as a corpse. Again, the virtue of the holy acts sprung from the body of a Brahmin is not, according to Brahminical theories, destroyed by the destruction of the body. Hence Brahminhood cannot consist in the body.

"Is it learning that constitutes Brahminhood? If that were the case, many Sudras must have become Brahmins from the learning they possessed. Many Sudras, even *Mlechchas* were masters of the four Vedas, of Vyakarana and Jyotisha, of the Mimamsa and the Vedanta, and of Samkhya, Nyaya and Vaisheshika philosophies; yet not one of them was ever called a Brahmin. Nor can *achara* and *karma* be said to constitute Brahminhood. For many Sudras are everywhere following practices appropriate to Brahmins, and are performing the severest and most laborious acts of piety.

"Why then should the higher life be prohibited to the

Sudra? Why is it laid down that for the Sudra service and obeisance to Brahmins are enough? Is it because in speaking of the four castes the Sudra is mentioned last? How can the order in which certain beings are named or written affect their relative rank and dignity? Does the Sudra become the lowest and meanest of beings, because his name is mentioned after the dog in a certain Sutra? Are the teeth superior in dignity to the lips, because we find the latter placed after the former for the sake of euphony in some grammatical rule? No; nor any more is it true that the Sudra is vile and the Brahmin high because we are used to repeat the *chatur vama* in a particular order. And if this is untenable, the inference from it that the Sudra must be content to serve and obey the Brahmin falls likewise to the ground.

"Again, if, as the Brahmins say, all men proceeded from one Brahma, how then could there be a four-fold insuperable diversity among them. If one has four sons by one wife, the four sons, having one father and mother, must all be essentially alike. Among quadrupeds, birds, trees, we see differences of confirmation and organization, whereby we can separate them into distinct species. But all men are formed alike without and within, except in such non-essential differences as are observed in the children of one and the same parents. It is therefore evident that all men belong to one species. Further, in the jack tree the fruit is produced from the stem, the joints and roots as well as the branches. Is one fruit therefore different from another so that we may call that produced from the roots the Sudra fruit? Surely not; nor can men be of four different species, because, as the Brahmins assert, they sprang from four different parts of one body. Besides, a Brahmin's sense of pleasure and pain is not different from that of a Chandala. Both are born in the same way, both sustain life in the same manner, and both suffer death from the same causes. They differ neither in intellectual powers nor in their actions, nor in the aims they pursue, nor in their subjection to fear and hope. Accordingly the talk of four castes is fatuous. All men are of one caste."

The reign of Kanishka terminated about A.D. 123. Very little is known of his successors. The last of the Kushan line was Vasudeva I, whose coins exhibit on the reverse the figure of Siva (?) with his attendant symbols. After the death of Vasudeva about A.D. 178 no paramount power seems to have existed in Northern India. Probably several princes asserted their independence and formed a number of short-lived states. About A.D. 308 a local Raja near Pataliputra, bearing the name of Chandragupta, was raised by matrimonial alliance with the Lichchavis to such dignity that he presumed to call himself *maharajadhiraja*. He extended his dominion along the Gangetic valley as far as the junction of the Ganges and Jumna. He was succeeded by his son Samudragupta who increased his dominions by many wars of aggression. His dominion extended from the Hooghly on the east to the Jumna and Chambal on the west and from the foot of the Himalayas on the north to the Narmada on the south. Though in his youth Samudragupta was a pupil of the great Buddhist teacher Vasubandhu, yet being an orthodox Hindu he carried out a horse sacrifice *(asvamedha)* with great splendour to proclaim the universality of his dominion. His son was the great Chandragupta Vikramaditya who, though tolerant of Buddhism, was an orthodox Hindu, specially devoted to the cult of Vishnu, and therefore bent upon preserving the observance of the rules of caste. Fahien, the earliest Chinese pilgrim, visited India during this reign and was favourably impressed with the position of Buddhism in India. He says: "Throughout the country no one kills any living thing, or drinks wine, or eats onions or garlic. They do not keep pigs or fowls, there are no deelings in cattle, no butcher's shops or distilleries in their market places." A son of Vikramaditya ascended the throne in A.D. 413 and like his grandfather celebrated a horse sacrifice.

Though the Gupta emporors were tolerant towards Buddhism, yet they were officially Brahminical Hindus, guided by Brahmin priests and patronizing the sacrificial rites abhonent to Buddhist sentiment. During this period there was on the whole a recrudescence of Brahminical Hinduism. But the tolerant spirit of the kings and the new development of Buddhism in its Mahayana form necessitated a readjustment of the Brahminical theories without the renunciation of any of the claims already set up for the born-priest. The new form of Buddhism, with its Sukhavati, Amitabha, Bodhisattvas, with its castelessness and emphasis on devotion and compassion, was better fitted to call forth the reverence not only of the casteless foreigners but also of the unlettered classes of the Hindus, especially the upper divisions of the Sudra caste, the so-called *Sacchudras*. Further the personality of the Buddha, who is represented in the various legends, the so-called *Jatakas*, as enduring infinite trials through numberless ages and births, foregoing the right to enter Nirvana for the sole purpose of teaching mankind the way of salvation, liberation from sorrow and suffering, exercised a great charm. There was no such figure in Vedic Hinduism. Moreover, the sacred literature of the Buddhists was open to all without distinction of caste or creed. But the Brahminical Vedas should not even be heard by the non-*dviga*. The Buddhists had a *dharmasastra* suited to all classes in the *Mahavastu*. Should not the Brahmins devise something to make up for these defects? No wonder that the *Mahabharata* under went a recasting and attained its modern shape.

Whatever may have been the original motive of the *Mahabharata*, there can be no doubt that the existing version is the result of a revision at the hands of the Brahmins of the Gupta court for sectarian and caste purposes. "The fact that the *Mahabharata* is the same in Bengal and in Southern India, in the Panjab and throughout the Dekkhan, shows that it was carefully edited with a set purpose and is not, as the superficial reader might imagine, a corpus of Brahminical literature strung together haphazardly in different periods of time." In its present form it is not only an encyclopaedia of mythology, philosophy, history and the sacred law, but it has also the status of a "fifth veda" and a "dharmasastra," intended specially for the unlettered Sudras. While the Vedas could not be repeated in the hearing of the Sudras, the *Mahabharata* could be read and explained to them. What was the necessity for a *fifth* Veda? To cope with their Buddhist rivals the Brahmins must have some book which could be accessible to the non-*dviga*. The old epic tradition had great influence on the popular mind. Much didactic matter, calculated to impress upon the people and their kings the theories of the priestly caste, was incorporated into the epic, and a book which contained about twenty four thousand verses was developed into one containing a hundred thousand verses. Thus the epic was made to assume the character of a vast treatise on duty *(dharma)*, in which the divine origin and immutability of Brahminic institutions, the eternity of the caste system, and the subordination of all to the sacerdotal class, were emphasised. But some concessions were also made to the non-*dviga*. It is declared that a Sudra may become *asamskrito dvigah* hereafter and that he should be revered (*senyah*) like a regenerate person, if he is "pure of heart and of subdued senses," since "not birth, nor sacrament, nor learning, nor stock (*santatih*) makes one regenerate, but only conduct" is the cause of regeneration. What Brahminism, pure and simple, teaches in regard to the Suara is clear from the Brahmanams and the Dharmasutras, and we do not find this teaching even in the Upanishads. It is pure Buddhism taught as Brahminism. But it would be too much for the Brahmins to admit unreservedly, as Sakyamuni did, that all men could free themselves from sin and attain the status of a Brahmin. That would be only setting a premium on the teaching of the great Kshatriya reformer. Hence the *Mahabharata* openly exalts the Brahmins and covertly dissuades the members of the other castes not to follow the teachings of the Kshatriya Sakyamuni.

The influence of the Kshatriya teacher on the popular mind was very great. He was regarded by all his followers as one born to take upon himself the sins of all mankind, "the endurer of ills for the benefit of existing beings". A new Kshatriya teacher had therefore to be fabricated to displace Sakyamuni from the high regard shown to him. A deity, possessing Kshatriya traits, was ready to hand and he was anthropomorphised. Agni and Indra were the favourite deities of the Vedic pantheon. Agni was the Brahmin among the gods and was the household deity of the priests. In later days he came to be worshipped as Rudra, who according to a Brahmana text was born out of a heap of the most frightful substances made by the gods to punish the creator Prajapati for committing incest with his own daughter, their sister. The Kshatriyas among the gods were Indra, Varuna, Soma and so on. Indra is the most important among them, as is indicated by the fact that about two hundred and fifty hymns celebrate his greatness, more than those devoted to any other god. He is the king of heaven. He gives victory to his people and is always ready to take in hand the cause of his servants and is therefore the good protector. He fights his great battles for the deliverance of the waters, the cows, the spouses of the gods, kept captive by the demons. As a god of heaven he is also the dispenser of all good gifts, the author and preserver of all life. He can take many shapes. He is not always moral. He is an adulterer and is not above practising deceitful wiles even without the justification of a good end. Vishnu is Indra's friend and ally; he is Upendra. We read in the Brahmanams: "See you the deeds of Vishnu, whereby he beheld the sacred ordinances, Indra's allied friend. Indra, forsooth, is the deity of the sacrifice, and the sacrificial stake belongs to Vishnu." "And as to why the oblation is one for Indra and Vishnu, it is because Indra raised the thunderbolt and Vishnu stood by him." "The Riks and Samans are Indra, and the Yajus are Vishnu. And by means of these Yajus they, as it were, bring forward that Vishnu, the sacrifice." "Agni is the lower half and Vishnu is the upper half of the sacrifice." "Indra and Agni are the whole universe." "Indra is the self (soul) of the sacrifice." "Now Indra and Agni were created as the Brahmin and the Kshatra: the Brahmin was Agni and the Kshatra Indra. When created the two were separate: They spoke, 'Whilst being thus, we shall be unable to produce creatures; let us both become one form?' The two became one form." "Now he who is this Vishnu is the sacrifice." The identification of Vishnu with Indra is not difficult. Vasudeva and Govinda are the names of Indra that were transferred to Vishnu. In the Rig Veda epithet Gopa (- protector of cows) is applied to Vishnu, and with this are connected the names Govinda, Gopala, Gopendra. According to the same Veda the highest step of Vishnu is the dwelling of the "many horned swiftly moving cows." The *Mahabharata* itself says: "Assuming the form of the sun (Vishnu's head) I cover the universe with my rays. And because I am the home of all creatures, therefore am I called by the name of Vasudeva." In the Bodhayana Dharmasutra Vishnu is called Govinda and Damodara. The ancient worship of Indra is referred to in Sanskrit and Tamil literature. In Panini there is a reference to the ancient worship of Arjuna which is the mystic name of Indra. Megasthenes speaks of the worship of Herakles, and no Brahminic deity resembles Hercules more than Indra, whose achievements bear great resemblance to some of the twelve "labours" of the former. Out of the rain-giving god Indra was evolved the dark-blue god Krishna and invested with all the qualities of Mara, the enemy of Buddha.

Adolf Holtzmann asks: What fatality impelled the Indians to elevate such a character into an incarnation of the supreme deity? Similarly Prof. A. B. Keith asks: "How comes it that we have in the Epic the picture of the most immoral Krishna, a cunning trickster, the evil genius of Arjuna and the Pandavas? In the tribal god of a rude agricultural or pastoral people these traits do not surprise greatly, for man makes gods in his own image, but what an extraordinary fate for the preacher of a pure and elevated monotheism." The answer is found in the following taken from the *Bhagavata Purana*: "The transgression of virtue and the daring acts which are witnessed in superior beings must not be charged as faults to these glorious persons......But let no one other than a superior being ever even in thought practise the same......The word of superior beings is true, and so also their conduct is sometimes: let a wise man observe their command which is right......Since Munis are uncontrolled and act as they please, how can there be any restraint upon him (the supreme deity) when he has voluntarily assumed a body?" So the incarnation of the supreme deity, though preaching morality, is not expected to act morally in accordance with his teachings. The Brahmin, being an opportunist, has never set much store by morality. He could always resort to the casuistry of *apatdharma*. Here was an enemy who must be circumvented somehow. A Kshatriya must be raised to the position of a deity, and the ideas adopted from the enemy must be so adapted and transmuted as to make them look indigenous and original. The Buddhists regard a Buddha as a man born to save the human race from impending ruin, whenever sin and ignorance gain the upper hand in this world. In the *Saddharmapundarikam*, a sacred book of the Mahayana Buddhists, the Buddha says: "I am the Tathagata, the Lord, who has no superior, who appears in the world to save." Similarly Krishna is made to say: "Whenever there is a decay of *dharma* and there is a rise of *adharma*, then I manifest myself. For the protection of the righteous and the destruction of the unrighteous, for the firm establishment of *dharma* I am born in every age." *Dharma* does not here mean religion in a Christian or Buddhistic sense but only in a Brahminic sense. As Samkara points out, religion here means only such religion as is indicated by castes and religious orders. In the proem to his commentary on the *Bhagavadgita* Samkara says: "When, owing to the ascendancy of desire in its votaries, religion was overpowered by irreligion, caused by the decreasing faculty of discrimination, then it was the original Creator (*Adikarta*) Vishnu, known as Narayana, desirous of maintaining order in the universe, incarnated himself as Krishna, begotten in

Devaki by Vasudeva, for the preservation of the 'earthly Brahmana', of the class of Brahmins on the earth. For it was by the preservation of the class of Brahmins that the Vedic religion could be preserved, since on that class all distinctions of caste and religious orders depended." It is therefore natural that, against the Kshatriya teacher who denounced the system of castes and the superiority of the born-priest, the Brahmins should set up another Kshatriya, though he be only an anthropomorphised god, to teach the Hindus to worship the Brahmins and follow the rules of caste.

In the mouth of this god Krishna, who is identified in the *Matsya Purana* with Kama, are put the ideals contained in the *Bhagavadgita*, which is described as the essence of all *sastras* and all *Upanishads* (*sarvasastrasara, sarvaupanishadsara*) and has been given the status of an *Upanishad* under the name of *Gitopanishad*. While the real *Upanishads*, which form a part of the Vedas, cannot be read or heard by the Sudra, this *Gitopanishad* which forms a part of the *panchama veda* can be read and heard by him. The burden of this "Song of the Exalted One" is apparently the exhortation to do one's duty in this life without attachment. But underlying this overt exhortation to do one's own duty, to be true to oneself, not to avoid the work which has been ordained for each by nature, there is a defence of the system of castes. The situation in which the defence of caste is advanced is well chosen. The hostile armies of the Pandavas and the Kauravas are facing each other in the field of Kurukshetra, which had already become famous as the place where the gods had performed a great sacrifice. Arjuna, the famous archer of the Pandavas, who had already subdued the whole of Jambudvipa, catches sight of his grandfather Bhishma, his teacher Drona, and others whose lives he valued in the army of the enemy The thought of killing them shocks him and he lets his bow and arrows fall, preparing rather to die than fight under such conditions. His charioteer Krishna admonishes him to discharge his duty. So the god in human form demands the fulfilment of duty. But what is one's duty? How is Arjuna to decide between the comparative claims of conflicting duties? In the mind of Arjuna there is a conflict of duties, a conflict between the dictates of his conscience and the duty imposed by caste rules. Lord Buddha taught that every one must decide for himself according to the best dictates of his reason and conscience what his duty shall be.

But Sri Krishna tells Arjuna not to give way to the noble sentiments of love and affection which move him to desist from fighting but to follow the duty imposed on him as a Kshatriya, just in the same manner as Samkara defends the killing of animals in sacrifices on the ground that such killing is enjoined by the Vedas, although it may be opposed to the sentiment of humanity. No doubt an attempt is made to give the system of castes a more tenable basis. For the old doctrine that to attain salvation the members of the other castes should first become Brahmins by going through a series of births, the *Gita* substitutes a new doctrine that "man attains salvation, devoted each to his own duty" and that the duties of Brahmins, Kshatriyas, Vaisyas and Sudras are determined by their natural qualities. "The four-fold castes were instituted by me according to the distribution of energies (*guna*) and actions (*karma*)." "Of Brahmins and Kshatriyas and Vaisyas, as also of Sudras, the duties are divided according to the qualities born of nature." "Serenity, self-restraint, austerity, purity, forgiveness, and also uprightness, knowledge, experience, faith——these are the duties of the Brahmanas, born of nature." "Bravery, boldness, fortitude, dexterity, and also not fleeing from battle, generosity and lordliness are the duties of Kshatriyas, born of nature." "Ploughing, cattle rearing, and trade are the duties of Vaisyas, born of nature; the duty of the Sudra which consists in service is also born of nature." "Devoted each to his duty, man attains prefection." "Better one's own *dharma*, destitute of merit, than the *dharma* of another well performed. He who does the duty ordained by his own nature incurs no sin." "Nature-born duty, though faulty, one ought not to abandon, for undertaking to do another's duty is fraught with evil (*naraka*.") "And would it be well for me to be the author of the confusion of castes and destroy these beings?" "Those men whose steps are not guided by the family or caste *dharma*, stray of a truth into the darkness of hell and rarely set out of it." "So, having an eye to the solidarity of society, thou shouldst perform thy duty." "As the ignorant act from attachment to action, so should the wise act without attachment to preserve the solidarity of society." "Let no wise man unsettle the minds of ignorant people attached to action." It is evident from these passages that the *Gita* aims covertly to support the domination and prestige of the Brahmin class, while appearing to provide for the wants which Buddhism satisfied. In Buddhism only works of unselfish love, characterised by absolute detachment (*upekshā*), can lead to *nirvana*. "The world is fettered by works," says the *Gita*, "save in the work that has for its end the sacrifice. Work to this end do thou fulfil, O son of Kunti, free from attachment." Whatsoever is noble and sublime in the *Gita* is what Brahminism has freely borrowed from its rival and utilised for its own purposes, especially to prevent the Sudras from seceding from their old faith. The rest is a conglomerate of repetitions, contradictions, absurdities, the result of an unsuccessful attempt to reconcile all phases of orthodox opinion.

The emphasis laid in the *Bhagavadgita* on killing as a duty calls to mind the following tradition that the Chinese traveller Yuan Chwang heard concerning Dharmakshetra, otherwise called Kurukshetra:—"The five Indies" were once divided between two sovereigns who fought for mastery invading each other's territory and keeping up unceasing war. At length in order to settle the question of superiority, and so give peace to their subjects, the kings agreed between themselves to have a decisive action. But their subjects were dissatisfied and refused to obey their kings' commands. Thereupon the king (of that part of India which included Thanesvar) thought of an expedient. Seeing it was useless to let his subjects have a voice in his proposals, and knowing that the people would be influenced by the supernatural he secretly sent a roll of silk to a clever Brahmin commanding him to come to the palace. On his arrival there the Brahmin was kept in the inner chamber, and there he composed (that is, by the king's inspiration) a Dharmasutra (that is, a treatise on duty). This book the king then hid in a rock cave, where it remained for several years until vegetation covered the spot. Then one morning the king informed his ministers at an audience that he had been enlightened by Indra, who told him in a dream about an inspired book hidden in a certain hill. The book was brought forth, and officials and people were enraptured. By the king's orders the contents of the scripture were made known to all, and the sum of them was briefly this.

"Life and death are a shoreless ocean with ebb and flow in endless alternation; intelligent creatures can not save themselves from the eddies in which they are immersed. I have an admirable device for saving them from their woes.

and it is this.—Here we have 200 li round this city the place of merit for generations of the ancient sovereigns, but as its evidences have been effaced in the long lapse of time, people have ceased to reflect on the efficacy of the place, and so have been submerged in the ocean of misery with no one to save them from perishing. Now all who, being wise, go into battle and die fighting, will be reborn among men: slaying many they will be innocent and will receive divine blessings: obedient grand children and filial children serving their parents while sojourning in this district will obtain infinite happiness. As the meritorious service is little and the reward it brings great, why miss this opportunity? Once the human body is lost there are three states of dark oblivion; hence every human being should be diligent in making good *karma,* thus all who engage in battle will look on death as a return home.—Then the king ordered an enrolment of heroes for battle and an engagement took place on this ground. The bodies of those killed in battle were strewn about in confused masses, so great was the number of the slain, and the huge skeletons of these heroes still cover the district which popular tradition calls the place of Religious Merit." Thomas Waters, from whose translation of Yuan Chwang's Siyuki this passage has been taken, remarks that "it reads like an extract from the Bhagavadgita." Here probably lies the reason of the incorporation of the *Bhagavadgita* in the revised version of the *Mahabharata.*

The gospel of duty has been preached very often. A gospel of duty devoid of content can not have any practical value. The sense of duty must get its subject matter somewhere. It is but natural that a gospel of duty seeking its content should readily lend itself to the idealization and consecration of such specific duties as the existing social order might prescribe. In a society subject to the regime of castes what caste commands becomes the congenial outer content of a purely inner sense of duty. Ideal justice comes to be treated as taking a practical shape in the form of caste. Caste is thus made to represent exactly the incarnation of ideal law. To him who abides strictly by what caste imposes on him are promised the benefits of the observance of an ideal law. We might even say that caste demands self-sacrifice in so far as it constrains one to act, not according to one's natural aptitudes or desires, but according to the caste in which one is born. This self-sacrifice is devotion to the kingdom of the

Absolute on earth. Hence the necessity of a philosophy of the Absolute as a supporting back-ground for this practical philosophy. Any philosophy which is not consistently *a posteriori* will always traffic in Absolutes, however much they may differ in form. But let us not forget that philosophical absolutism is no less dangerous than political absolutism. Philosophical absolutism has no regard for happiness as a test of action, and those that profess it have an unfortunate way of living up to their principles by making others unhappy. In all absolutist philosophies the good of society appears in the whole rather than in the individuals taken severally. The high role played by the society as a whole is taken as compensating the misery of individuals. The whole society dictates functions to every individual, and the law of justice is that he should do what his special duty demands, however hard or humble may be the place so assigned. Since in the end the individual's true nature lies beyond his visible self, any claim to better oneself becomes blasphemy. Since the *summum bonum* consists in removing the illusion (*maya*) which makes it seem unaccomplished, each individual must find by asceticism and renunciation his true sphere and genuine reality in the Absolute Self. Thus all incentive to reform and progress is cut off at the very root, and a justification is provided for caste inequalities, slavery and the ignorance and prostration of the masses. All absolutist philosophies, owing to the emphasis they lay on the relation between the individual life and the universal life, tend to withdraw men from social relations. In fact, the general effect of absolutist philosophies on the world has been "mainly to sap intellectual and moral sincerity, to excuse men in their consciences for professing beliefs which on the meaning ordinarily attached to them they do not hold, to soften the edge of all hard contrasts between right and wrong, truth and falsity, to throw a gloss over stupidity and prejudice and caste and tradition, to weaken the basis of reason and disincline men to the searching analysis of their habitual ways of thinking." All the six orthodox systems of Hindu philosophy, namely, Samkhya, Yoga, Nyaya, Vaiseshika, Mimamsa and Vedanta, maintain some form of Absolute or Absolutes, and therefore overtly or covertly support the system of castes.

Philosophical absolutism is an absurdity. The Absolute

is defined as something out of relation to known things. How could any such existence be established by reasoning? Existence itself means the capacity of producing an effect and implies therefore relation to other things. We know nothing absolute; all is relative. Nothing is even cognisable, thinkable, expressible which is not a relation. Language itself is a system of relations. There is no action without the relation of cause and effect, of antecedent and consequent. All abstraction implies relation. There is no time without relation between two phenomena. There is no space without a body in space. There is no reality without someone capable of perceiving it. Two terms are always necessary. Even when I think of myself, my sentiments, my sensations, there is always something that is not I. If I should desire to know myself pure and simple, freed of all foreign elements, it would be necessary to isolate myself from all my sensations and sentiments, from all that which, in my thoughts, has language for its origin. Consider a man born blind, deaf, incapable of tactile sensation, and hence deprived of all relation with the material world and his fellow beings. Such a man, not to speak of his being conceivable, would know nothing; in return he would have absolute knowledge, that of identity between the knowing subject and the object known: it is I knowing I. Such is the Absolute of metaphysics. The Absolute at first is the I, then it is I penetrating into all things, becoming their consciousness, and finally knowing them all as the I knows itself by complete identification with all. *Aham brahmasmi, tatvamasit.* By this magical operation man is supposed to apprehend the basis of all things, the thing in itself. This operation, which is a special kind of vertigo or autohypnosis for the suppression of consciousness, is called *Yoga* and is described in the *Bhagavadgita* thus: "A devotee remaining in a secluded place should always devote his mind to contemplation, alone with his mind, self-restrained without any expectations, and without any concern, fixing his seat firmly in a clean spot, neither too high nor too low and spreading over it a piece of cloth, deer skin and *kusa* grass, there seated in one spot and his mind fixed on one point, and restraining mind and senses, one should practise contemplation for the purification of his self, holding his body, head and neck perfectly still and fixing his eyes on the tip of his nose and without looking in any direction." The disappearance of cognition thereby produced is regarded as absorption of consciousness into the Absolute (*sakshatkara, samyagdarsana*). One can easily lapse from consciousness into unconsciousness, but to dub nescience as super-consciousness and rank it as something above consciousness capable of revealing the underlying nature of all things, is only to make oneself proof against criticism at the sacrifice of the right to a respectful hearing.

In the *Gita* an attempt is made to connect a man's beliefs, sentiments, modes of life and actions with the Samkhya theory of the three *gunas.* The three guna . are named *sattva, rajas* and *tamas.* Though they are not present in their entirety anywhere, there is no part of the universe where at least a minimum of these is not to be found. In the period of dissolution of the universe they slumber. But the actions of *souls,* not recompensed in the previous age of the universe, awaken them into being and make them proceed upon a new evolution. When in the course of evolution human beings and particular products have come into existence, the three *gunas* maintain throughout the universe an unceasing struggle for supremacy. If the several constituents are allowed to develop freely, *sattva* is manifested in the world of objects as light and buoyancy and in man as virtue, benevolence, happiness, cheerfulness, &c.; *rajas* is manifested as force and movement in the world of objects and in man as every kind of suffering, anxiety, passion, wickedness, &c, and also as ambition, effort and activity; *tamas* is manifested in the objective world as heaviness, rigidity and darkness, and in man as cowardice, fear, stupidity, sloth, &c. According to this theory *sattva* predominates in the world of the gods, *rajas* in that of men, *tamas* in that of animals, plants and minerals. Mankind also are classified into their divisons, Brahmin, Kshatriya, Vysia, Sudra according to the predominance of one of these *gunas.* "There is no being on earth, or again in heaven among the *devas* that can be free from these three *gunas* born of *prakriti.* Of Brahmins, Kshatriyas and Vaisyas, as also of Sudras, the duties are divided according to the qualities born of nature. Serenity, self-restraint austerity, purity, forgiveness, and also uprightness, knowledge, experience, faith——these are the duties of the Brahmin, born of nature. Bravery, boldness, fortitude, dexterity, and also not flying from battle, generosity and loneliness are the duties of Kshatriyas, born of nature. Ploughing, cattle-rearing and trade are the duties of Vaisyas, born of nature;

the duty of the Sudra which consists in service is also born of nature. Devoted each to his own duty, man attains perfection." One is a Brahmin, Kshatriya, Vaisya, or Sudra not by training but by natural endowment. Consequently the status of a man in the scale of caste is determined by birth and cannot be altered. As the theory of *gunas* traces the characteristics of men to physical causes, it must naturally lead to fatalism and asceticism. The whole theory is a fanciful hypothesis in which no part can find any support in modern science.

The struggle between Brahminism and Buddhism is really a struggle for the maintenance of the rule of caste and the supremacy of the Brahmin. Though according to the Brahminical theories the Kshatriya and Vaisya share with the Brahmin the privilege of reading the Veda, yet that privilege extends only so far as the Veda is taught and explained to them by their Brahmin preceptor To the Brahmin alone belongs the right of teaching and expounding the sacred texts. Hence in the view of the Brahmins the greatest sin of Sakyamuni was that, he, being a Kshatriya, transgressed the duties of his own class by assuming the function of a preceptor and the right to receive gifts, which the Brahmins regarded as their exclusive privilege; and worse still he instructed the members of the fourth caste whom the Brahmins placed outside the pale of instruction. This is exactly the charge which Kumarila Bhatta brings against the Buddha in his *Tantravartika*. "What confidence can we have," says Kamarila, "that one who being a Kshatriya, transgressed the duties of his own order and assumed the function of a teacher and the right to receive presents would inculcate a grave system of duty? For it has been said: 'Let every man avoid a man who practises acts destructive of future happiness. How could he who ruins himself be of any benefit?' And yet this very transgression of Buddha and his followers is conceived of as being a feather in his cap; since he spoke thus: 'Let all the evils resulting from the sin of Kaliyuga fall upon me; and let the world be redeemed.' Thus abandoning the duties of a Kshatriya, which are beneficial to the world, assuming the function of a teacher which belongs only to the Brahmins and instructing men out of the pale in duty enjoined to the Brahmins, he sought to do a kindness to others, while consenting to violate his own obligations; and for such merits as these he is praised! And who follow his instructions, acting in contravention of the prescriptions of the *Sruti* and *Smriti*, are notorious for their erroneous practices."

In the *Sankaravijaya*, ascribed to Madhava, we are told that the gods, strongly impressed with the religious corruption prevalent in the world, repaired to Kailasa and addressed Mahadeva thus: "The earth is now overcrowded by the Bouddhas, who put faith in the doctrines of Buddha and vilify the orthodox philosophies. The enemies of Brahminism hate the regularities of caste and orders, and speak of the Vedic texts as merely meant as livelihood for the priests. No man ever performs the *sandhya* and other ceremonies, nor the *samnyasa*. All are become heretics. They close their ears immediately on hearing any one speaking of sacrifices. How then can religious rites go on, how can we enjoy the fruit of sacrifices? What religious text is there, referring exclusively to the supreme being, that has not been mauled by the besotted Bouddhas? Other systems, too, there are on earth, full of mischief, to which men resort and come to misery. Therefore do you destroy all wicked people, and for the protection of mankind, establish the Vedic system so that the world may become happy." Mahadeva promised to grant the prayer of the gods, and by way of commencing work at once addressed himself to his son Kartikeya. Mahadeva told Kartikeya that the gods Vishnu and Sesha had already become incarnate for the purpose of saving the Upasana Kanda from destruction; that he himself proposed to appear on earth as Sankaracharya to rescue the Gnana Kanda, but before he did so Kartikeya should take upon himself the human form and preserve the Karma Kanda. He instructed Kartikeya thus: "Descending to the earth, fix all regulations in accordance with the Vedas, after overcoming all Saugatas (Bouddhas) who are enemies of the teaching of the Vedas. And in order to help you Brahmadeva will become a Brahmin Mandana and Indra a king named Sudhanvan." After the preliminary arrangements are concluded in heaven, the scene changes to the earth and we are told that Indra becomes a model king in this world and Kartikeya appears at his court as Kumarila Bhatta "having acquired fame in elucidating the true teaching of the Vedas expounded in the Sutras of Jaimini and defeats the Saugatas in argument. But to prove the truth of the doctrine he preached, he falls down a steep hill unhurt and converts a snake into Vishnu. Then the king is satisfied and issues an order for the destruction of the Bauddhas. About this king Sudhanvan Dr. G. U. Pope says that the Tamil equivalent of this name (strong bow or good bow) is Val-vil-ori or Athan-ori, one of the seven generous celebrated chieftains of the old Tamil lyrics. Those lyrics date generally from the fourth to the eighth century A.D., and therefore embrace the period of Kumarilabhatta. It is just possible, therefore, that Val-vil-ori and Sudhanvan may be identical, though we have no evidence to support the theory. This king was according to the poems a mighty hunter, his chief residence being a hill called Kolli, on the Malabar coast, a place from which the Chera kings take one of their titles In this connection it may be noted that the *Kerala Utpatti* states that the Buddhists were driven out of Kerala by Kumarila Bhatta, so that the locality in question tallies with both legends.

To maintain his supremacy the Brahmin has resorted to all means. Wherever he had special royal patronage, the casteless Buddhists were persecuted. We have already referred to the destruction of many monasteries by king Pushyamitra. According to the Buddhist tradition there were three persecutions of the faith between the times of Nagarjuna and Asangha. During the reign of Skandagupta the Hun deluge burst upon India. Though their first assault was repelled by Skandagupta (A.D. 465), yet the Gupta empire finally succumbed to its foes. The Huns under the leadership of Toramana subjugated the north-west and made Sakala in the Panjab their capital. Toramana was succeeded by Mihirakula. Mihirakula was a worshipper of demons and their head Siva. He bitterly and cruelly persecuted the Buddhist monks, destroyed the Buddhist *stupas* and monasteries and plundered them of their treasures. Narasimhagupta Baladitya, who is described by Yuan Chwang to be an ardent Buddhist, seems to have overthrown the Huns in a decisive battle and driven Mihirakula to take refuge in Kashmir. After this dispersion of the Huns there is a gap in our knowledge for a century till we come to the reign of Harsha Siladitya. Harsha Vardhana was a staunch supporter of Buddhism, and his sister, after the death of her husband, became a Buddhist *bhikshuni*. King Harsha prohibited the slaughter of all living creatures within his dominions and enforced all his people to abstain from flesh-eating, himself setting the example.

The partiality for a vegetarian diet which characterises the Hindu of the present day is the result of the work of Asoka and Siladitya. Brahminism has had no share in it. In all Brahminical sacrifices the remains of the animal slaughtered had to be eaten. Manu declares that the man who, having in due form performed a (*m*[illegible]*thuparka* or other) rite, fails to eat flesh meat, will be doomed to be born an animal for twenty generations. The *Mahabharata* bears testimony to the high value of flesh as an article of diet. Bloody offerings are still common in many of the temples of Northern India. Nevertheless, we find in the mouth of every Hindu the well-known saying *ahimsa paramo dharmah*. How has this change been brought about? We can not say that it is wholly due to a natural disposition to benevolence. For we find a learned and thoughtful Brahmin like Samkara defending the *jyotishtoma* sacrifice as a holy act, though it involves the shedding of blood, on the ground that the sacrifice is enjoined by the Vedas as a duty. The real reason of the change of feeling towards bloody sacrifices is given by the author of the *Nirnaya Sindhu*. This writer says: "The slaughter of large bulls and large sheep for Brahmins versed in the Vedas, should not be effected being detested by the public. Further the rule, let a cow fit for offering to Mitra and Varuna, or a barren cow, or one that has ceased to bear after first calving be sacrificed, is duly ordained, but such sacrifice, being opposed to public feeling, could not be performed." What could have been insturmental in producing this revulsion of public feeling against the ordinances of the Vedas, were it not the denunciation of the slaughter of animals by such Buddhist kings as Asoka and Harsha Siladitya? The Buddhist appeal to humanity was so strong that it created a horror against the vain sacrifice of animal life, which even a belief in the authority of the Vedas and the Smritis could not overcome.

Like other Buddhist kings Harsha Siladitya was a liberal patron of other religions. Yuan Chwang has given an account of the great Buddhist festival at Kanouj in A.D. 644, to which all the feudatories of the empire were summoned. The festival at Kanouj was followed by another great ceremony at Prayaga where the king gave all his wealth to the poor and those devoted to religion. On the first day an image of the Buddha was set up, on the second day that of the sun, and on the third day that of Siva, an indication that a fusion was gradually taking place between Buddhism and other religions. In the distribution of gifts the Buddhist *bhikshus* took precedence. After them the Brahmins were honoured, then came the Jains and other sectaries for their share, and lastly the wants of the poor and destitute were satisfied. The favours bestowed by king Harsha on the Buddhists appear to have excited the jealousy of the Brahmins so that they not only set fire to the temporary lofty tower built for the image of the Buddha at Kanouj, but also made an attempt on the king's life. Yuan Chwang states that the investigation that followed these two untoward incidents led to the banishment of five hundred Brahmins convicted of being accomplices. The enemy of Harsha, Sasanka, king of Western Bengal, did his best to extirpate Buddhism. He uprooted the sacred Bo-tree at BuddhaGaya and laid waste the adjoining sanctuaries and monasteries. Orthodox Brahminism seized the opportunity of Harsha's death to assert its political supremacy. Arjuna (or Arunasa), one of Harsha's ministers, set aside the claims of Harsha's family and put himself on the throne. Arunasa insulted and maltreated the envoy from the court of China where Buddhism was in the ascendant. But Wang-hieuen-tse, the leader of the mission, together with his deputy, escaped to Nepal, and with the help of armies placed at his disposal by the Buddhist kings of Nepal and Tibet, soon overran Magadha and made Arunasa captive and returned to China.

The Gupta princes who ruled in East Magadha after the break up of Harsha's empire were succeeded by the Pala kings who were devout Buddhists. Like all zealous Buddhists the Pala kings were very tolerant of other religions and even bestowed gifts upon the Brahmins. But the Sena kings, who reft away the eastern portion of the Pala territory, were intolerant. A century after Yuan Chwang visited India, the Brahmins were brought to Bengal with the object of spreading Brahminism and suppressing its great rival. The Sena kings were the great allies of the Brahmins in their endeavours to secure both these objects. The Sena kings used to grant lands to Brahmins in perpetuity in close proximity to Buddhist monasteries. The Buddhists were ridiculed in poetic compositions and execrated in public. The very sight of a Buddhist was considered an occasion for performing expiatory ceremonies. Ballala Sena enforced the rules of caste and gave succour to Kulinism. He drove away the

Sonar Banias, who were Buddhists, from his dominions. Those who remained in Bengal were degraded and Brahmins were prohibited from teaching them and officiating in their religious ceremonies. Both the Pala and Sena dynasties were brought to a sudden end by Mohammed Bhakhtiyar Khilji. All the intellectual followers of Buddhism were either massacred or compelled to fly away from the country. Buddhism was practically stamped out from Bengal. Owing to the Mohammedan invasion the Brahmins who lived on the lands granted to them by the Pala and Sena kings lost their lands and other sources of income. They were compelled from this time to extend their activity as priests. Such of the Buddhists as consented to become their submissive followers were admitted by the Brahmins into the fold of Hindu society and called the *navasakha* or the new branch. Those that tried to maintain a separate existence were declared *anacharaniya* or untouchable classes. A large number of the Buddhists, like so many lambs without a shephered, were converted to Islam either by force or by persuasion. It is not improbable that the social philosophy of the Prophet of Islam which, like the teachings of the Buddha, gives all believers an equal spiritual status, better suited the Buddhists than Brahminism which teaches that "the wealth that is stolen by the Brahmin tends to well-being in the next life, the wealth that is given to the Sudra tends only to hell" and that "immoral Brahmins are to be worshipped, but not Sudras though subduing their passions, as the cow that eats things not to be eaten is better than the sow of good intent."

How Buddhism fared under Brahminic sway is best shown by a study of the Buddhist community in Nepal. The Gurkha government throws its favours and influence on the side of the Hindus. The casteless Buddhists are ostracised as *anacharaniya* and put outside the pale of the Brahminic community. The king acting under the advice of the Brahmins may make some particular families or classes into clean castes. In Nepal at the present time there exists among the Buddhists a sort of distinction between the priestly and the non-priestly occupations. But the distinction is not so pronounced as in Brahminic society. When Bengal was a Buddhistic country, a similar distinction was observed among the several classes of the Buddhists. After the Mohammedan conquest Brahminic ideals were superimposed on the Buddhistic ideals of society. The distinctions among the classes became more and more prominent, till they developed into a regular caste system. Forgetting their past history the people came to think with the Brahmins that all distinctions were due either to cross-breeding or to excommunication. The survivals of forgotten Buddhism became the *anacharaniya* class.

It is a mistake to suppose that Hinduism is not a proselytising religion. Only its method is different from that of the three universal religions of the world. Hinduism proselytises by its system of castes. People who do not observe the rules of caste are *mlechchas*. *Mlechchas* become Hindus or Brahminists by accepting the system of castes and the Brahmins as their spiritual guides and by venerating the cow and attributing purificatory efficacy to its urine and dung. Any number of outsiders may be brought within the fold of Hinduism so long as they are willing to form themselves into a new caste without interfering with the existing castes and to submit themselves to the spiritual authority of the Brahmins and invite them to all ceremonies and pay them. It was in this way that the casteless foreigners, like the Sakas, the Yuechi, and the Huns, succumbed to the absorptive power of Brahminism and became Hinduised. "Clans or families which succeeded in winning chieftainship were readily admitted into the framework of Hindu polity as Kshatriyas or Rajputs, and there is no doubt that the Parihara and many other famous Rajput clans of the north were developed out of barbarian hordes which poured into India during the fifth and sixth centuries. The rank and file became Gujars and other castes, ranking lower than the Rajputs in the scale of precedence. Further to the south, various indigenous, or 'aboriginal', tribes and clans underwent the same process of Hinduised social promotion, in virtue of which Gonds, Bhars, Khanwars, and so forth emerged as Chandels, Rathors, Gaharwars and other well-known Rajput clans, duly equipped with pedigrees reaching back to the 'sun and moon'." It is inevitable that an endogamous community, trying to secure spiritual sway over other communities, should group them into a hierarchy by means of castes. While child marriage is least prevalent among the hill tribes almost uninfluenced by Brahminism, it exists in undisputed sway or in a mixed form among the tribes whose social life derives its main characteristics from the caste system of the Hindus. By imitating the customs and practices of the

Brahmins the lower classes ascend in the social ladder. Some have done so by introducing child marriage and others by prohibiting widow remarriage.

The marriage of girls before puberty and the prohibition of the remarriage of widows are the direct result of the system of castes. The widow has to remain a widow for the purpose of the annual *sraddha*, the ceremony which assures repose to the *jiva* of her dead husband. According to the Hindu theory of marriage when a woman marries the husband receives from her father or guardian the proprietorship of the woman. Therefore conformably to the rites the second marriage of a woman could not be effected in the absence of the proprietor of the woman who alone had the right to transfer his property. Behind these religious reasons lie also certain utilitarian grounds. All the families which compose a caste have a common advantage in prohibiting the remarriage of widows; these experienced women may prove unfair competitors of young girls who already do not find it easy to get husbands. As has been already stated the fear of impure alliances has made endogamy the rule. But when a caste becomes divided into a number of sub-castes, then a regular hypergamy becomes established. For example the Rashi Brahmins of Bengal are divided hierarchically into Kulins, Siddha-Srotriyas, Sadhya-Srotriyas and Kashta-Srotriyas The Kulin can marry in his own sub-caste and in the two higher sub-castes of Srotriyas; the Siddha-Srotriya in his own sub-caste and in the sub-caste of Sadhya-Srotriyas, but the Sadhya-Srotriyas and Kashta-Srotriyas can exercise their choice only within their respective sub-castes. If the young Kulin Brahmins can marry equally in the inferior sub-castes or in their own sub-caste, evidently the young girls of this sub-caste will have fewer aspirants for their hands. As the possibilities of choice for the male members of a sub-caste outside their own caste become greater, the chances of getting husbands within a sub-caste for its female members become smaller. Hypergamy must naturally lead to either the early marriage, or the perpetual maidenhood (as among Nambudris), of the girls of the higher castes. Thus the collective instinct has led to the interdiction of widow remarriage and to the early marriage of girls. But even when such customs might not be vitally necessary for a caste, the desire to imitate the twice-born castes and thus rise in prestige extends the area over which these pernicious customs prevail. While courtship and marriage between adults is the rule among tribes that have not been influenced by Brahminic civilization, child marriage is found among tribes whose social life derives its character mainly from the caste system of the Hindus. The attempt to find a support for the Brahminic practice of early marriage in Freud's theories of psycho-analysis is no better than the attempt to find an antiseptic basis for the Brahminic use of cow dung as a purificatory agent.

If any *anacharaniya* community changes its priests for Brahmin priests, the community with its gods and goddesses are taken within the fold of Brahminism. The doctrine of *avataras* enables the Brahmin to enrich his pantheon with new deities. The Buddha, who was a sort of Anti-Christ for the Brahmins, has become one of the ten *avataras* of Vishnu. It is not unlikely that the Buddha came to be looked upon as an *avatara* of Vishnu in Hinduised Buddhist circles. The oldest work with a fixed date in which the Buddha is represented as an *avatara* of Vishnu is Kshemendra's *Dasavatara charita*. In this book the ninth incarnation of Vishnu is spoken of as the son of Suddhodana and Mayadevi. Amarasimha, the Buddhist author of the *Amarakosa*, knows the Buddha as the son of Suddhodana and Mayadevi, but does not speak of him as an *avatara* of Vishnu. It was in the interval of time between these two authors that the fusion between Buddhism and Brahminism took place which led to the inclusion of the Buddha in the Brahminic pantheon. In places where Buddhism still prevailed, the Brahmin could not mask the figure of Buddha. So in the *Nepala Mahatmya*, the guide of the Brahmin pilgrim in Nepal where Buddhism still exists in a degraded form, the Buddha is assigned an equal rank with Siva and Vishnu, and Parvati, the wife of Siva, teaches that "in this incomparable country to adore Buddha is to adore Siva", and special rites are prescribed in honour of Buddha. Similarly in the *Nilamata Purana*, which is the canonical authority of the Brahminical cult in Kashmir, where Buddhism prevailed for a long time, the birth-day of the Buddha as an incarnation of Vishnu is celebrated on the full-moon day of the month of Vaisakha, which is the anniversary of the birth of the Buddha in all Buddhist countries. This Purana even asks the faithful to set up and worship the image of the Buddha with the recitation of the verses employed by the Sakyas and also to worship the latter and present them with food, garments and books. In the calendars of modern Kashmir the Buddha's birth-day still retains a place. But in places where Buddhism had no intellectual leaders, the Brahmins have resorted to fraud and endeavoured to make out that Vishnu took the form of Buddha to deceive the enemies of the Brahmins. The *asuras*, the enemies of the Brahmins, had, it would appear, by the rigorous observance of Vedic rules and rites, become more powerful than the Brahmins themselves, a state of affairs that could not be tolerated, and therefore they induced Vishnu to assume the form of Buddha and preach to the *danavas* the futility of Vedic rules and rites. A careful study of the stories about the ten incarnations discloses that they were a device adopted by the Brahmins to secure for themselves the high position they have gained in the estimation of other Hindus. It would be a dangerous precedent to admit a Kshatriya to the rank of a Brahmin. But there could be nothing unsafe or inconvenient in promoting a Kshatriya to the rank of a god, especially together with other Kshatriyas who taught the worship of Brahmins and cows. Though the Buddha image in the Mahabodhi temple at Buddha-Gaya, now in the possession of a Hindu *mahant*, is worshipped as the Buddha-avatar of Vishnu, yet the real attitude of Brahminism towards Buddhism is well seen at the same place, where the Hindu pilgrims to the adjacent Brahminical shrines are seen scowling and even spitting upon the Buddhist images now conserved there by the Government. Indeed the Gaya pilgrimage which every pious Hindu must perform is one of direct hostility to Buddhism, the great GayaAsura, whose suppression is the *raison d'etre* of the pilgrimage, being none other than Buddha himself. This gives the lie to the view of some that Buddhism disappeared from India by amicable amalgamation with Brahminism. Not satisfied with all that has been done in antagonism to Buddhism, the Brahmin expects that the first expedition of the coming tenth avatar of Vishnu, namely, Kalki, will be against the Bouddhas of Kikata, where, according to the *Bhagavata Purana*, Vishnu incarnated as Buddha, the son of Anjana, for the purpose of deluding the enemies of the gods on earth.

Diverse have been the methods employed for the maintenance of the system of castes. Kumarila Bhatta championed sacerdotal Brahminism by resuscitating the doctrine of works (*karma marga*) by a commentary on the *Purvamimamsa*. For the acceptance of sacerdotal rites they should be based on indubitable authority. Human authority not being infallible, it was necessary for the *purvamimamsaka* to establish the infallibility and superhuman origin of the Veda. His work was supplemented by Sankaracharya, who endeavoured to attack Buddhism on its philosophic side. In doing this he accepted the teachings of *Gaudapada karika*. This *karika* contains verses which appear to be only extracts from a work of the great Buddhist teacher, Nagarjuna, and employs against the realistic Samkhyas and Vaiseshikas the very same arguments as were employed by the Buddhist *vignanavadins* and *sunyavadins*. It also taught that all things in the world were the product of illusion. All duality is said to be mental (*dvaitam sarvam manas*). So long as the mind is at work, there is a knower, knowing, and the known. In sleep, on the other hand, there is no object for thought and consequently no duality. In deep dreamless sleep Brahmam "knows" itself. "It is a knowledge where there is nothing to know and no knower". The individual soul is neither a part nor a production of Brahmam; it is Brahmam itself. How is this to be known? Certainly not by inferential reasoning, for Brahmam is not a self arising from any duality or from any reality of individual existence. Hence the existence of Brahmam must be accepted solely on the authority of scripture. But the knowledge of scripture presupposes a long course of training, a previous discipline according to prescribed rites. Hence the gates of higher knowledge are closed both to women and Sudras, who have been born so in consequence of evil deeds in past lives. Hence the Sudra, even if he have the intellectual and moral capacity, has not the 'spiritual' capacity arising by birth, and accordingly true knowledge can never present itself to him. And "as long as true knowledge does not present itself, there is no reason why the ordinary course of secular and religious activity (as manifested in the castes) should not hold on undisturbed." Thus was established the reality of the world of ordinary belief (*vyavahara*), and the necessity of winning the world from Buddhism to Brahminism, from castelessness to caste. Though it was necessary to become one with Brahmam, it must be accomplished by the founding of Brahminical monasteries (*mutts*) on the lines of Buddhist *viharas* and the restoration and preservation of Brahminical institutions. Samkaracharya's primary object was to root out Buddhism from the country, and to attain that end he countenanced every form of

Hinduism, including the worship of Siva, Sakti, Vishnu, Sun and Ganesa.

It is interesting to note that the Madhvas represent Samkara as an incarnation of Manimat, who, according to the Mahabharata, was a leader of certain *rakshasas* killed by Bhima. The *asuras*, we are told, despatched Manimat to incarnate as a Brahmana ascetic and destroy the Vedanta under cover of explaining it by establishing the identity of the individual soul with Brahmam. Manimat is born as a widow's bastard, named Samkara, and is brought up in great poverty. After going from teacher to teacher he invents his doctrine, described as *sunyamarga* and *nirgunatva*, and is hailed by the *asuras* as their saviour. On their advice he joins the Buddhists and teaches Buddhism under cover of Vedantism. Samkara's *Maya* doctrine is declared by the Madhvas to be Buddhism in disguise (*prachchanna bouddha*). Some scholars suggest that this Manimat theory of the Madhvas might have been due to the presence of Manichaens in the neighbourhood of the birth place of Madhvachari, the founder of the Madhva faith. Manichaens sometimes used language which implied that the soul was identical with the divine element. Mani represented the Buddha as the communicator of a divine revelation, and Manichaeism has much in common with Buddhism. Samkara is supposed to have received his education in Saurashtra, which was the region in which the Vignanavada and Sunyavada forms of Buddhism largely prevailed. With this view of Madhvas may be compared what the *Padmapurana* puts into the mouth of Siva: "It is I who, in this *kaliyuga*, taking the form of a Brahmin, have preached the doctrine of illusion (*mayavada*), a false doctrine, which is only disguised Buddhism, a doctrine condemned by men, and which disfigures the meaning of the words of the scripture. I have proclaimed this grand doctrine of illusion, as if it conformed to the Veda, though it is non-vedic, with a view to cause the destruction of beings."

A fact of some significance in the life of Samkara is his adoption of the life of a *sanyasin* without passing through the *grihastha* (householder) stage. This is a violation of the *asrama dharma* which we find generally coupled with *varnadharma* or the caste ideal. According to the *asrama* rules one has to pass in succession through the stages of *brahmacharya*, *grihastha*, and *vanaprastha* before entering upon *sanyasa*. His violation of the *asrama* rule was patent to Samkara himself, as he apologises by saying that the *asrama* rule was not observed in his day. But we doubt if the *asrama* rule was ever observed strictly by the Brahmins. Apasthamba, one of the law-givers, says that there is no reason to place one *asrama* before another and condemns the life of a *bhikshu* by quoting a saying of Prajapati that those who become *bhikshus* do not attain salvation, but become dust and perish. Again, another law giver, Boudhayana, quotes another old saying that an *asura* made the *asramas* striving against the gods and therefore a wise man would not take heed of them. These indicate that the Brahmins were never keen about the *asrama* ideal. This ideal was evidently introduced as a protest against the practice, obtaining among the Buddhists and the Jains, of youths becoming *bhikshus* without passing through the life of a *grihastha*. The *grihastha* stage was necessary for the continuance of the born Brahmin and a male descendant was necessary for the worship of the spirits of the dead (*pitris*). The *asrama* ideal is therefore not the inheritance of the Brahmin from his ancient forbears, and has no right to be spoken as *sanathanadharma*. But all things are equally old for mendacious gabblers.

When the Brahmin immigration to South India took place we are not in a position to decide. Asoka sent missionaries to the country of the Cholas and Pandyas as well as the Satiyaputra and the Keralaputra. Buddhism flourished for a long time in South India. From the beginning of the first century to the beginning of the third Buddhism flourished vigorously in the Telugu country. The famous Buddhist tope at Amaravati near the Krishna river was built under the rule of the Andhra-Bhrityas. Tiruppappuliyur, now called old Cuddalore, was the capital of a Pallava province and the seat of a Buddhist University. Kanchi was a strong-hold of Buddhism and very recently Buddha images were discovered in the *pradakshana* part of the Kamakshi temple there. It is said that in the eighth century a Jain teacher from Sravana Belligola, named Akalanka, who had been partly educated in the Bouddha college at Ponataga (near Trivalur), disputed with the Buddhists at Kanchi in the presence of the last Bouddha prince, Hemasitala, and confuted them, that the prince became a Jain, and that the Bouddhas were banished to Kandy. Vara Pandya of Madura, on becoming a Jain, is said to have persecuted the Buddhists, subjecting them to personal tortures, and banishing them from the country. A relative of Udaya Varma, the head of the Chola Royal family and king of Northern Kerala, became a Buddhist and built several temples and lived apart from the royal family. Bhatta Kumarila who lived at the end of the seventh century regarded the South Indian dialects as *mlechcha* or un-Brahminic, as they were the languages employed by the Buddhists. It would therefore be not too much to assume that about 700 A.D. Brahminical civilization had but little penetrated into South India. The Brahmins might have begun to find the south a promising field of labour, but there were very few settlers. Yuan Chwang who visited Kanchi speaks of the inhabitants as chiefly consisting of Jains and some Buddhists, but has not a word about Brahmins. The title of *ayyar* or "father" given to the Brahmin in South India indicates his position as a missionary and founder of a new order among a people uninfluenced by Brahminism. He is therefore a new comer; and hence no Brahmin in India is more bigoted and exclusive, and less willing to permit the inferior castes to rise in the social scale. Unlike the Brahmin of the north there is no lower caste from whose hand he will take water. The reason assigned is that Hinduism in the north has been defiled by successive foreign conquests, while, isolated in the south, it has remained untouched by foreign influence.

The Hindus at the present time may be divided into two large groups, the Brahmins and the non-Brahmins. The castes which describe themselves as Brahmins, however exclusive they may be among themselves, follow for the most part the religion taught by the Smritis, while the castes, not calling themselves Brahmins, generally follow the religion of the Puranas. The Puranas are all post-Buddhistic, as they all speak of the Buddhavatar and one of them specially speaks of Suddhodana's son who beguiled the *daityas* to become Buddhists. In most of these works there are large sections on the rights and duties of the different castes, on the different *asramas*, and on general Brahminic rites such as *sraddhas*. Nearly all the Puranas are sectarian in character, that is to say, they are devoted to the cult of one of the deities, Vishnu and Siva, and describe the ceremonies and feasts (*vratas*) and the places of pilgrimage (*tirthas*) relating to the one or the other. The theory of Yugas finds a full exposition in them and is connected with the caste system. The word *Yuga* occurs in the Vedas and the names of the four Yugas, *Krita*, *Treta*, *Dvapara* and *Kali*, occur in the Brahmanams.

But these words originally belonged to the language of the gamblers of the Vedic times. *Treta* meant three; *dvapara* meant two; *krita* and *kali*, meaning respectively "accomplished" and "strife", represented four and one respectively. So they represented the figures cut or engraved on the dice. But the word Yuga in the sense of a cycle or age is post-Vedic. It is in the Puranas and the laws of Manu that we find the theory of the four Yugas coupled with the theory of the three Gunas in full bloom. In the same books occur the texts on which has been based all that is objectionable in caste. One of the Puranas definitely assigns the origin of caste to the Treta Yuga: "The perfect beings of the first age, some tranquil, some fiery, some active and some distressed, were again born in the Treta, as Brahmins, &c., governed by the good and bad actions performed in former births". A bull was introduced in the Puranas as a symbol of the Vedic religion. In the Krita Yuga, the glorious age of all excellence, this bull stood on four legs; in the Treta, the age of knowledge, one of his legs was broken; in the Dvapara, the age of sacrifice, two legs were broken. In the present age, the Kali Yuga, the age of darkness, three of his legs are broken and the bull is limping on the remaining leg. The fact that the Buddha is described as having made his appearance in the interval (*sandhya*) between the Dvapara and Kali Yugas indicates how the bull happened to lose its legs. So the theory of the one-footed Kali is merely the attempt of the Brahmin to explain away the disrepute into which the Vedic ritual had fallen. As already mentioned the revivalists of Hinduism had to fight not with a ritualistic religion but with a form of Buddhism in which *bhakti* or devotion to the teacher (*guru*) played a dominant part. The Vedic ritual deliberately kept the Sudra at a distance. So in the Puranas, intended largely for the use and edification of the *non-dvijah*, is emphasised the doctrine of *bhakti* in the form of devotion to one or the other of the gods, Vishnu and Siva. The readiness displayed in the Puranas to provide relief from sin and enable every one to obtain substantial blessings in a future life shows that Brahminism found it expedient to smooth the path of religion for the masses outbidding other claimants for popular favours. Whether deliberately provided or not, the easy ways of gaining final emancipation provided by the Puranas must have presented better attractions than the self-discipline demanded by Buddhism from its adherents. It is not improbable that the popular teachings contained in the Puranas served to absorb the Buddhists into Hinduism. The essential difference between Brahminism and Buddhism is the worship of gods and the worship of *gurus*. All Hindus at the present day worship both *devas* and *gurus*, and the *guru* is looked upon as the living embodiment on earth of the god worshipped. This worship of *guru* by the various Hindu sects is nothing but the result of the influence of Buddhism on Brahminism.

Religion, even the most rudimentary, if it has not lost its vitality, represents the totality of knowledge to which the intelligence of a people has led them. It contains necessarily some explanation of nature, of the phenomena of which man, though he is the spectator and perhaps the victim, is conscious of not being the author. This is the part played by deliberative reason in the genesis of religions. If man aspires to know the forces of nature, the causes of the effects he perceives, it is because he desires to have some hold on them, of making use of them, of defending himself against them, in short, of finding some means of getting into practical relation with them. To conceive these forces as properties inherent in matter, as mechanical actions which occur regularly according to invariable laws, a long experience and an effort at abstraction, of which the primitive man is incapable, are necessary. He therefore makes the world in his image, that is to say, just as his acts are to him the result of his will (*atman*), so natural phenomena are the result of the intervention of wills incorporated in matter, but distinct and separable from the visible or tangible realities. All religions have to pass through this phase of their development, which is called *animism*, and, in reality, even those that have passed this stage are spoken of as religions, only when they possess some tincture of animism. Progress in religion consists in reducing the number, or banishing the presence, of these wills; in separating them from matter and creating for them an independent personality, while giving them at the same time power to act on nature, of which they form an integral part; and in grouping them in a hierarchy and placing at the top a supreme will. This is certainly the last stage in the animistic religions. What is called monotheism, or simply theism, is in reality only a system in which the multiple capricious wills of primitive demonology are subordinated to the will of an all-powerful being. When these subordinate agents who execute the orders of the omnipotent being and put him in relation with the world, are renounced, this being becomes relegated to an ineffable and inaccessible singleness. Then the transcendent being either becomes a metaphysical entity, conceived as an immutable will, showing itself in an implacable predestination, which, suppressing all freedom, renders prayer meaningless; or becomes immanent or infused in nature as its soul, being multiple in manifestation but at the same time one in reality. In this pantheism all diversity is reduced to appearance, and human personality affirmed by consciousness, is nothing more than a mirage floating on the ocean of the infinite all.

On the soil of India the development of religion has not been different. Examples of the different phases of development can be found among the various religions which are included under the term "Hinduism". From the demonology of the lower classes of Hindus to the metaphysical religious philosophy of Samkara it may be a far-off step. But all of them have one characteristic in common, perhaps the only characteristic, namely, the caste sentiment which underlies the social edifice. This sentiment forms the spinal cord of every religion described as Hindu. Even when the doctrines and ritual of any sect are incapable of providing it with vitality, it is the caste spirit that gives it strength and support. The bulwark of caste which the Brahmin threw round himself for the maintenance of his supremacy has resulted in a spirit of narrow exclusiveness which has infected every religion born on the Indian soil, as the following survey will show.

The most marked feature of the religion of the Rig Veda is henotheism, which naturally developed at a later stage into a monotheism. The development of one deity gradually into all deities and finally into the head of all is easy. Most probably this development took place in relation to the worship of the sun. In one verse of the Rig Veda the sun is called "the life (*atman*) of all that moveth and moveth not," and in another verse it is said of the sun: "They call him Indra, Varuna, Agni, and he is the strong-winged Garutman. To what is one (*ekamsantam*) wise men give many names; they call it Agni, Yama, Matarisvan." It is said that Yagnavalkya refused to obey his preceptor's command to join in worship with people whom he styled 'miserable and inefficient Brahmins'. He explained that he acted for *bhakti*, then departed and worshipped the sun. Even at the present day the sun is worshipped by Hindus as *surya bhagavan*, and some do not touch food unless they see the sun. All the legends connected with the Bhagavata religion are connected in some way or other with the sun. In later times the sun became identified with Rudra-Siva or Vishnu. Perhaps this coalition was due to the winning over of the Bhagavatas by the Vedic priests as their allies to stem off the propagandist work of the Buddhists. This monotheistic development gave rise to a new path of salvation, called *bhakti marga*, as distinguished from *gnana marga* and *karma marga*. In the *karma marga* the means to salvation consist of the observance of orthodox rites and ceremonies, while in *gnana marga* knowledge or philosophy forms the means. *Bhakti* first developed in Buddhist circles. The venerable Sariputra says: "Lord! Such faith have I in the Exalted One, that methinks there never has been, nor will there be, nor is there now any other, whether *sramana* or *brahmana*, who is greater and wiser than the Exalted One." The Mahayana brought this *bhakti* or devotional side of Buddhism to the forefront. It laid stress upon winning peace (*santi*) by *punya*, the passionate devotion of self to works of charity and love, rather than by *gnana*, the attainment of spiritual knowledge.

The example of right living and right thinking set by generations of the Buddha's devout disciples had been the source of inspiration to many religious teachers. The Buddha has two distinct characters. In his first and early character he is the typical *yogi*, the great teacher of the power to be gained by self-suppression and conquest of the passions. In his second he is the great friend of the common people, advocating universal brotherhood, universal equality, and universal compassion for all forms of animal life. In Rudra-Siva the Hindu revivalists found a suitable counterpart to the first side. The cult of Rudra-Siva is no other than the cult of Agni in its frightful aspect. The solemn and awful ceremony of the Satarudriya shows that Rudra became the representative of the fearful aspect of life and nature. No wonder that some *saiva* sects are horrible and demoniacal and they have developed Rudra into the horrid god Bhairava with his wife Chandika wearing a garland of human skulls and requiring human sacrifices and offerings of wine for his propitiation. Kashmir gave birth to a more humane and metaphysical system of Saivism. The *saiva* propagandists of South India were saints and poets rather than philosophers whose names are remembered only by their devotional lyrics. Though the Brahmins were the chief leaders and exponents of this movement, yet the majority of teachers were non-Brahmins, a feature due to the earlier introduction of Buddhism and Jainism in the southern country. The Saivites had to contend very largely with the Jainas and the influence of Jainism on Saivism seems to be evident in some of the stories of the Saiva Puranas and in the number sixty three of the devotees of Siva, which is also the number of the Salaka-purushas of the Jains.

An important Saivite sect in South India is the Lingayat or Virasaiva sect. The Lingayats went further than any sect of the Hindus in their reform. They set up for themselves a special system of social relations and domestic rites. They denied the supremacy of the Brahmin and received sacraments from their own priests. They discarded the cremation of the dead, the observance of caste and the laws relating to defilement, which are accepted by the other Hindus, such as those occasioned by a woman's periodical ailments and by the death of relations. They did not believe in metempsychosis, and consequently had no *tithis*, or anniversary festivals, to commemorate the dead and to afford them the benefit of the prayers, sacrifices and intercession of the living. They allowed their widows to remarry. In short, they regarded themselves as a community distinct from all those that owed their origin to the Brahminic system. According to Dr. Fleet the present Lingayat sect is a development of the guild of the five hundred swamis of Aihole, a village in the Bijapur District, the protectors of the Vira Bananju religion, who, though always Saivas, patronised also Buddhism. The members of the Virasaiva sect carry on their bodies the image of Siva in the form of *lingam*. Though this lingam is generally supposed to represent Siva's organ of generation, yet it is not unlikely that we have in this emblem of Siva a replica of the Buddhist *dagoba* with a Hindu interpretation behind it.

The fusion between Buddhism and Saivism is so complete that most of the ceremonies, practices and divinities of Saivism have their counterparts in Tantrik Buddhism. Buddha is said to be the brother-in-law of Siva. In Nepal on the 8th day of the month of Kartik Pasupati is decorated with a head-dress like that of the image of Buddha and worshipped. The *Siddhars* of Tamil literature are in no way different from the Siddhas of Mahayana literature. Like the Buddhists they are also not favourably disposed towards caste. In both Saivism and Buddhism the *tantrik* rites are connected with the doctrine of Sakti. In the ritual proper of the Saktas there are no caste differences and men of all castes become Brahmanas during the worship of the Bhairavichakra, though they resume their own castes when the worship is over. All castes are equally capable of attaining the goal (*Siddhi*). Both systems have a strong predilection for Yoga, by which the *mahasukha*. the joy of which *Sakti* is the organ, is to be obtained. The Sakta religion in all its forms freely resorts to intoxicants. For the drunken consciousness is regarded as a bit of the mystic consciousness, and the ecstacy of the latter is not essentially different from the former. "The sway of alcohol over mankind," says Prof. James, "is unquestionably due to its power to stimulate the mystical faculties, usually crushed to earth by the cold facts and dry criticisms of the sober hour...Not through mere perversity do men run after it. To the poor and the unlettered it stands in the place of symphony concerts and of literature; and it is part of the deeper mystery and tragedy of life that whiffs and gleams of something that we immediately recognise as excellent should be vouchsafed to, say, many of us in the fleeting earlier phases of what in its totality is so degrading a poisoning." But the pity of it is that the effects of intoxicants are habit-forming and the habit-forming nature of alcohol usually wins in the end, notwithstanding the great precautions taken to meet its poisonouss action.

Just as the *bhakti marga* found expression in various Saivite sects, so did it also show itself in Vaishnavite cults. The doctrine of the Vaishnava school is a qualified non-duality (*visishtadvaita*) like that of the Kashmir school of Saivism, Vishnu taking the place of Siva and Lakshmi that of Sakti. Vishnu is the Buddha in his character of a beneficent protector, and the Buddha is an incarnation of Vishnu. The majestic head of Vishnu which forms the centre of the figure of Trimurti is the Brahminical counterpart of the head of the Bodhisattva. Sir W. W. Hunter says in his *Indian Empire*: "If we examine the religious life of the Vaishnavite community, we find that their rules are Buddhistic with Brahminical reasons attached". It may not be easy to establish the truth of Hunter's statement. Yet there are features which bring Vaishnavism into close relationship with Buddhism.

Of all places sacred to the Vaishnavites the greatest is Puri. The *Purushottama Mahatmya* speaks of *chaturmurti*—Jagannatha, Balarama, Subhadra and Sudarsanachakra. The word Jagannatha is used more by the Buddhists as an epithet of the Buddha than by the Hindus as an epithet of Vishnu. The symbol of the Buddhist triad, Buddha, Dharma, Samgha, with a slight alteration, forms the figure which represents Jagannatha, Balabadhra and Subadhra in the Puri temple. In ancient sculptures and drawings Jagannatha is given as the ninth incarnation of Vishnu. Outside the gate of the holy city is to be found an emaciated figure of *Ekadasi*, the personification of the fast on the 11th day of the moon so sacred to Vaishnavas all over India, but she cannot enter Puri, as there the fast is prohibited. One of the essential features of Vaishnavism is thus neglected at Puri. The explanation is that Puri was a centre of Buddhism, and the Buddhists were opposed to fasting. The tradition is that the temple of Jagannath was built by Indra Dyumna, a Buddhist king who did not believe in castes. While other religions preach: "Fast and pray," Buddhism preaches: "Feed and meditate." No where is adoration paid to the discus of Vishnu. The importance attached to it at Puri and the fact of tho *Purushottama Mahatmya* making it distinct and of equal rank with the other three images, clearly shows that it had a Buddhistic origin. In Puri the throne on which the images are placed is called the *ratnavedi*, reminding one of the three *ratnas* of the Buddhists. Within the precincts of the temple of Jagannath at the present day no distinction is made between high and low castes, and the food prepared for the deity or dedicated to the images is received and eaten by all, and is supposed incapable of being polluted by the touch of the very lowest caste. In the *Gaya Mahatmya* there is a verse which enjoins that before offering the funeral cake on the Vishnu-pad the pilgrim should go to Buddha Gaya and salute the Bodhi tree there, which has to be saluted as the Bodhisattva in a special *mantra*.

The earliest of the Vaishnavite sects was that founded by Ramanuja. He was dissatisfied with his *advaita* teacher and separated from him. He came under the influence of Yamunacharya, the descendant of Nathamuni who had composed in Tamil songs of love and devotion to Vishnu. The *Prabandhas* or songs in praise of Vishnu are really the works of Brahmins, although they are ascribed to devotees of different castes, called Alvars. Ramanuja wrote nothing in Tamil. He wrote all his works in Samskrit. He gave an exclusive form to the path of salvation by *bhakti*. According to him the three upper orders, who alone were qualified to study the Vedas and to acquaint themselves with the *Purvamimamsa* and the *Uttaramimamsa*, could practise *bhakti*, but not the Sudras. However, the Sudras could practise *prapatti* by taking refuge (*saranam*) in a Brahmin devotee of Vishnu as preceptor (*guru*). Though a Samskrit Vaishnava verse says that a worshipper of Bhagavat is no Sudra, still the Sudra is not qualified to practise *bhakti*, because not being a *dvijah* he is utterly helpless. The followers of Ramanuja are divided into two schools, the Northern and the Southern. The former (*vadakalai*) teaches that a person belonging to an inferior caste should be treated on terms of equality only so far as conversation by words is concerned, while the latter school is more liberal and has shaped Ramanuja's teachings so as to include Sudras also. In the later years of his life Ramanuja was persecuted by the Saivite Chola prince of his time, and fled away from Srirangam to Mysore, where he converted one of the Jain princes to the Vaishnavite faith. The relations between the Jains and the Vaishnavites in Mysore do not seem to have been cordial. Even in Northern India when the Vaishnavites became more numerous than the Jains they persecuted the latter.

In the minds of many people there is a confusion between Jainism and Buddhism. But these two religions are poles asunder. Buddhism teaches that all asceticism is useless for attaining salvation, while Jainism teaches the absolute necessity of asceticism. Jainism represents a systematic development of the ascetic side of Brahminism. The Jains seem to take a sort of pride in outdoing their Brahminic rivals as regards rigorous conduct, mistaking nastiness and filthiness for the highest pitch of ascetic virtue, whereas the Buddhists endeavour to bring their conduct in accordance with the dictates of humanity. The doctrine of *ahimsa* degenerated in Jainism into an objection to the destruction of even the most infinitesimal insect life, and has led to ridiculous precautions against harm to such life or even to the air itself. The doctrine against the taking of another's property is carried to a prohibition of attachment to any object or person, even to the wearing of clothes. Jainism encourages religious suicide. Buddhism combats the Brahminic theory of the

Atman as being the absolute and permanent soul according to the pantheistic as well as the monadic point of view. But Jainism fully concurs in the Brahminic theory of the Atman. The Jains attribute souls not only to animals but also to the smallest particles of the elements. No such dogma is accepted by the Buddhists. The Jains are great sticklers for caste and have not been able to carry their religion beyond the limits of caste-ridden India. The Buddhists are to live, both in public and private, in the practice of those virtues which, when, unbroken, intact, unspotted and unblemished, make men free and which are untarnished by the belief in the efficacy of any outward acts of ritual or ceremony, or by the hope of any kind of future life.

A tangible way in which a religion shows its influence on civilization is art. From their contributions to art we can determine the inner natures of different religions. Buddhism, Brahminism and Jainism have each contributed in almost equal degree to the art of the cave temples of Ellora. Here we can follow with un-erring steps the underlying character of each religion. "In the earliest caves", says Sir John Marshall, the Director of the Archæological survey of India, "you see Buddhist art almost at its zenith; you mark its graceful lines; its rich but restrained decoration, its transparent sincerity, and above all its peace and tranquillity. You pass on to other caves. You see this same art slowly but surely declining under the deadening pall of convention; its creative force is stifled; it is becoming stiff, sterile and atrophied. You go further along the face of the cliff and enter another hall; at once you miss the intellectual and spiritual feeling of the earlier sculptures; around you are life-like figures starting from the rock—some solemn and majestic, others hideous and revolting, but all of them emotional, dramatic and awe-inspiring. You have passed from the realm of Buddhism into that of Hinduism, and you realise —with a start as it were—the vast gulf that separates the two. You can see forms obviously copied from the Buddhist; but their peacefulness is gone. *Ethos* (if I may use a Greek expression) has given way to *pathos.* They have become the incarnation of all the dead forces of nature, of passion and of lust, of suffering and death. And so you go from one to another of these halls, surrounded by sombre and relentless forms, peering from their dark recesses: you surrender yourself involuntarily to the prevailing gloom; but you do not, you cannot, forget the lofty spiritual beauty of the earlier caves; and you wonder within yourself what came over the spirit or the character of the people when they forsook Buddhism for the dread cult of Siva. And so you make your way, almost with a sigh of relief, to the temples of the Jains—all of them very perfect, all very elaborate, all very sumptuous, but one and all destitute of creative genius. You admire them for their rich decoration, but you can not help being struck with their narrow, nerveless design; and you gaze unmoved at their composed and icy images. It has always been so with the Jains." Taranatha declares that wherever Buddhism prevailed skilful religious artists were found, but where the *tirthyā* doctrines prevailed, unskilful artists came to the front. Similarly says Sir John Marshall that wherever the religion of the Buddha penetrated there the art of the Buddhists followed in its wake, and carried with it a message of lofty idealism and of spiritual grandeur unrivalled in the art of any nation. Brahminism had no art of its own in India and the plastic arts of Saivism and Vishnuism are the bastard children of the sculpture of the Buddhists. As Dr. Gunwedel says, "the figurative part of Brahman art, so far as we are now acquainted with it, is based essentially upon Buddhist elements--so much so indeed that the Saiva figures which originated at the same time as the Northern Buddhist, appear to have fixed types, whilst the iconography of the Vishnu cult embraces chiefly Buddhist elements to which different interpretation has been given. But still more dependent on Buddhism are the representations of Jaina art."

It is stated that a spirit of sympathy for the lower castes and classes of Hindu society has been a distinguishing feature of Vaishnavism. This certainly is not true of Ramanuja's religion. Although teaching the theoretical equality of all castes, if they are Vaishnavites, the teachers and leaders of the religion of Ramanuja have been invariably Brahmins. Ramanuja laid down the strictest injunctions as regards eating and drinking. The liberalising influence of Vaishnavism in South India was due not to Ramanuja but to some of his later disciples. It is interesting to note that in South India there is a class among the followers of Ramanuja known as *satanis*. The word *satani* is connected with the Samskrit word *satana* which means clipt hair. These Satanis have shaven heads and play a leading part in temple services and in the funeral ceremonies of non-brahmin Vaishnavites. It looks as if these people had originally no caste among them. Some try to trace them to Sanatana, a follower of Chaitanya, who travelled in the south. But their practices seem to indicate that they were originally Buddhists who, though accepting the teachings of Ramanuja, still stick on to their Buddhistic practices. Again, there is a class of Vaishnava mendicants called *dasaris* who seem to be invested with some sort of authority. No marriage or funeral ceremony among the non-Brahmin Vaishnavas takes place without their presence and the payment of fees to them. They form an essential accompaniment in the pilgrimages of non-Brahmins to Tirupathi. Is this also a vestige of the connection of non-Brahmin Vaishnavas with Buddhism? Among Brahmins it is only the Tenkalai Vaishnava widows that do not shave their heads. It is believed that this custom belongs to the low castes, the Jains and the Buddhists who supplied the original Vaishnavite converts. For an analogue to *prapatti* some turn to Christianity, but it can be seen in the Buddhist theory of *parivarta* or diverted merit. Ramanuja's system is known as Sri sampradaya, as Sri or Lakshmi, the wife of Vishnu, plays a dominant part in procuring salvation for man. It is interesting to note that the figure of Sri in South Indian sculptures resembles the figure of the nativity of the Buddha in the sculptures at Sanchi.

Though Ramanuja discarded Samkara's *advaita*, he still preached a doctrine of qualified non-duality, called *visishta-advaita*. According to this teaching the Brahman of the Upanishads is a personal God, in whom everything that is exists and who is endowed with every imaginable auspicious quality. Soul *(chit)* and matter *(achit)* alike proceed from God (Vishnu) and God pervades all things as their inward support *(antaryamin)*. The doctrine of non-duality in every form was rejected by Madvachari, who taught the doctrine of duality. He affirmed the existence of two separate eternal principles, instead of three, as taught by Ramanuja; these two principles are supposed to be related as independent and dependent, as master and servant, as king and subject. The independent principle is identified with Vishnu and the dependent principle with the human soul. The clerical members of Madva's sect are Brahmins, but the lay votaries are members of every class of society but the lowest. The followers of this sect are great sticklers for caste.

It is in the teaching and life of Ramananda that we for the first time meet with the strict observance of the equality of all castes. Ramananda was a disciple of Raghavananda, the head of the monastery founded by Ramanuja at Seringapatam. Ramananda had an altercation with his teacher on a question of discipline, and, going to Northern India, established there a sect of his own. Its principal doctrinal peculiarity consists in insisting on Vishnu in his form of Rama as the chief object of devotion. It may be pointed out that the whole story of the Ramayana is an adaptation of a Vedic legend. Sita can be traced to the Rig Veda where she appears as the furrow personified and invoked as a goddess. In some of the Grihya sutras she again appears as a genius of the ploughed field, is praised as a being of great beauty, and is considered the wife of Indra or Parjanya, the rain god. There are traces of this origin in the Ramayana itself. For Sita is represented as having emerged from the earth when her father was once ploughing, and at last she disappears underground in the arms of the earth-goddess. Her husband, Rama, is no other than Indra, and his conflict with Ravana, the chief of the demons, represents the Indra-Vritra myth of the Rig Veda. This identification is confirmed by the name of Ravana's son, Indrajit, or Indrasatru, the latter being originally an epithet of Vritra in the Rig Veda. Ravana's most notable feat, the rape of Sita, has its prototype in the stealing of the cows recovered by Indra. Hanumat, the chief of the monkeys and Rama's ally in the recovery of Sita, is the son of the wind god, with the patronymic Maruti, and is described as flying hundreds of leagues through the air to find Sita. Hence in his figure perhaps survives a reminescence of Indra's alliance with the Maruts in his conflict with Vritra and of the dog Sarama who as Indra's messenger crosses the waters of the Rasa and tracks the cows. Sarama recurs as the name of a demoness who consoles Sita in her captivity. The teachings of the Ramayana, like that of the Mahabharat, virtually consist in asking the Kshatriya rulers of the country to follow their great ancestor Rama and not to attach any importance to the revolutionary teaching of the son of the petty Kshatriya chieftain of the Himalayan Terai. By preferring the Rama avatar to that of Krishna, Ramananda introduced a purer and more chaste worship.

Unlike previous Vaishnavite teachers Ramanand wrote

in the vernacular instead of Samskrit, and thus brought his teachings within the reach of all classes. He also interpreted the *bhakti* doctrine of the brotherhood of man in its most liberal sense and admitted all castes, even the lowest, not only as lay members of his sect, but also as teachers. He released his followers from the shackles of caste, laying down no special ordinances as regards eating or bathing. Among his twelve chief disciples there were a barber and a low caste leather worker, each of whom founded a sub-sect. The liberalizing influence of Ramanand's teaching was the source of the religious revival in Maharashtra which covered a period of nearly five hundred years. This period gave birth to various saints and prophets from among all castes, even outcastes, who manfully struggled against the exclusive spirit of caste domination. Namdev was a tailor by birth as well as occupation. Ekanath, though a Brahmin, decried caste and suffered much in consequence. Chokamela was a Mahar. Tukaram, a contemporary of Sivaji, was a petty shopkeeper. All these asserted the spiritual dignity of man as being independent of the accident of birth and social rank. The result of this movement was the removal of caste exclusiveness from the religious sphere and its relegation to the social concerns of life. Some believe that the idol worshipped under the name of Vittala at Pandharpur, with which the popular Vaishnavism of the Mahratta country is connected, was originally an image of the Buddha. The image has a curious sort of crown, which reminds one of the *ushnisha* of the Buddha images. A novel institution of the *bhakti* movement of the Mahratta country is the *harikatha*, a popular exposition of religion in the form of story interspersed with song.

The Mohammedan conquest of India interrupted the course of evolution of religion in India. Mohammedanism or Islam believes in one god, who is supposed to have revealed his will to mankind through an Arab named Mohammed who died about 632 A.D. These revelations are contained in the Koran. The earliest method of propagation of the faith was persuasion, especially when the hearers showed signs of receptiveness. But from the eighth year of the flight of Mohammed to Medina, when a manifesto, demanding the submission of all mankind to the faith, was issued, Islam was propagated by the sword, and where the conquered were not forced to become converts they were reduced to a tributary caste. The humiliations and vexations to which the non-Moslem was put rendered life so intolerable as to compel conversion to Islam. The equality of all Moslems is a fundamental doctrine of Islam. If there was anywhere a caste system, it was due to the conquering power arrogating to itself all the offices of the state. As regards non-Moslems Mohammed's principle was to tolerate Jews and Christians but to exterminate others, who were called pagans. On the subject peoples of other cults Islam inflicted the disability to bear arms, as the orthodox teaching forbids the Moslems to have non-Moslem allies in their wars. Autocratic government is the characteristic of all Islamic states, a natural consequence of Mohammed's position as divine commissioner over his community. Islamic jurisprudence regards legislation as absolutely beyond man's capacity, his business being to administer according to rules revealed by God. The punishment for apostasy is death. Four obligations are incumbent on every Moslem: the repetition five times daily of certain formulae in Arabic accompanied by certain postures of the body; fasting during the whole month called Ramadan from sunrise to sunset; pilgrimage at least once in a life-time to Mecca followed by one to Medina; the apportionment of two and a half per cent of one's possessions, when one has means, for the support of the poorer members of the community. Of forbidden foods the most important is pork, and the drinking of wine also is prohibited, although this rule has been violated from the earliest times. Islam permits polygamy and furnishes great facilities for divorce. The immediate consequence of these privileges of the male sex was the seclusion of women and the use of the veil. One of the duties incumbent on the Moslem community is the *jihad*, the fighting of mankind in general to render Islam dominant. The Moslem should not remain on land which is not under Islamic domination, but quit it if he can not subdue it.

The earliest Moslem invaders of India waged ruthless war against Buddhism and Brahminism. The Mohammedans made no distinction between Brahminists and Buddhists and called them both by the same name Hindu or Indian. In the early period of their conquest they could not brook the neighbourhood of Hindus and therefore ruthlessly massacred all Hindus and destroyed their temples, although after permanent colonization they suffered idolaters to live in their neighbourhood. Alberuni says that Mohammed of Ghazni utterly ruined the prosperity of the country. In A. D. 1024 Mohammed penetrated Kattiwar and destroyed the famous temple of Somnath. Kutbuddin captured Benares, destroyed nearly a thousand temples, and raised mosques on their foundations. Alauddin sacked the temple city of Bhilsa, and sent the idols to one of the gates of Delhi to be trodden under the feet of true believers. Even Feruz, more merciful than his predecessors, forbade the erection of new temples, repressed all unbelievers, and imposed poll-tax (*jizya*) on all Hindus. Feruz was severe not only with the Hindus but also with Mussulman sectaries. Like Mohammed of Ghazni he was a zealous iconoclast, and as a good Sunni he burnt the books of the Shiahs and suppressed their propaganda. Feruz took great interest in the welfare of his proselytes, no matter how the conversion was effected. The invasion of Timur in 1398 A. D. was accompanied by massacre and rapine at Hardwar and other places. Sikander, the second of the Lodi dynasty, was a just ruler and patron of learning, but too zealous a Mussulman not to support the bigoted Sunnis in their quarrels with the Hindus. He not only destroyed Hindu temples, but built mosques opposite to bathing ghats and prohibited the Hindus from bathing there. Islam being an individualistic cult, is a protest against the restraints laid down by Brahminism on individual liberty. The social practices of the Hindus were therefore felt as an offence by Mussulman rulers, however much they might try to be just in their rule.

The contact of the stern monotheism of Islam with reformed Vaishnavism brought about some purely deistic developments which are observed in the teachings of Kabir and Nanak. In the religious history of India Kabir occupies an important place. He was a Mohammedan, but became a disciple of Ramanand and thus belonged to the Vaishnava school of thought. He attempted a fusion of Hinduism with Islam and the result was that some of his followers describe themselves as Hindus and some as Mohammedans. Kabir rejected entirely all the outward signs of Hinduism. He acknowledged no caste distinctions, saw no virtue in asceticism and fasting, and ruthlessly condemned the Hindu theogony. Transmigration was a feature in his doctrine borrowed from Hinduism. Though he employed the name of Rama, it meant for him only the supreme being and not the incarnation of Vishnu.

Nanak was a contemporary of Kabir and worked in the Panjab. His creed in its strict form enjoins the belief in a single god, condemns the worship of other deities, idolatry, pilgrimages to the great shrines of Hinduism, faith in omens, charms, and witchcraft; and does not recognise ceremonial impurity at birth or death. As a social system it abolished caste distinctions, and, as a necessary consequence, Brahminical supremacy and ordinances, in all family rites. The followers of Nanak are called *Sikhs* (from Samskrit *siksha*). The scripture of the Sikhs is called the *Adigrandh* and contains many sayings ascribed to Kabir.

The teachings of Kabir and Nanak influenced many earnest souls to protest against the grosser abuses in Hinduism. Dadu was one such person, who spent his life in preaching the new doctrines over the Midlands. He again and again said: "I am not a Hindu, nor a Mussulman. I belong to none of the six schools of philosophy. I love the merciful God." He rejected the Vedas and the Quran as ultimate truth, the Vedantic philosophy, ritualism and formalism, caste and caste marks, idolatry, the use of the rosary, pilgrimages and ceremonial ablutions. He held that the world was not evil in itself, but that the bad man made it evil by allowing it to lead his mind away from God. He gave a new interpretation to the doctrine of transmigration of souls by saying that all possible rebirths happen in man's one life on earth. "The moods of mind and the quality of actions give the soul the birth of a fox, a goose, a pig, an ass and such like."

In the fifteenth century under the patronage of the Sharki sultans Jaunpur, which was founded by Feruz Shah, became a great seat of Mohammedan learning. One of the sultans, Husain Shah, endeavoured to reconcile the religious differences of the Hindu and the Mussulman communities. By his orders the *Bhagavata Purāna* was first translated from Samskrit into Bengali. It may be pointed out that the Mohammedan conquest was instrumental in elevating the Bengali language to the status of a court language. As the Buddhists wrote in the vernaculars of the people, the vernaculars were looked down upon by the orthodox Brahmins. The historian of Bengali literature declares that "if the Hindu kings had continued to enjoy independence, Bengali would scarcely have got an opportunity to find its way to the court of kings". Hussain Shah originated a religious cult to unite Mussulmans and Hindus in the worship of one god under the hybrid name of *Satyà-Pir*, a word composed of the Samskrit word *satya* and the Arabic word *pir*. The Jaunpur school instilled a spirit which made it possible for pious Mussulmans to become the followers of Chaitanya and also prepared the way for the Din-Ilahi of Emperor Akbar.

For a long time the Brahmins did not reconcile themselves to the Mohammedan conquest. In the fourteenth century, however, began a reconciliation of the Brahmins with the ruling Mussulman powers. The Bahmini kingdom was established at Gulberga in the Dekhan by Hasan Gangu Bahmini, a servant of Gangu, a Brahmin astrologer of Delhi. He took the name of Bahmini in gratitude to his Brahmin patron and made the latter his finance minister. According to Ferishta this was the first time a Brahmin accepted office in the service of a Mussulman ruler.[1] Before that time the Brahmins were sometimes in favour with the ruling Mussulman sovereigns as astrologers, philosophers, physicians, but they held aloof from public affairs and never held official positions. After Gangu's time the Brahmins of the Dekkhan controlled the finances of Mussulman rulers. Religious animosities gradually diminished. A Brahmin minister served at the Mussulman court of Ahmednagar, and another acted as the confidential adviser to Amir Berid, who ruled at Bidar. This reconciliation reached its acme in the reign of Akbar, who was singularly free from all sectarian prejudices.

The attitude of the Emperor Akbar towards his Hindu subjects was entirely different from that of his predecessors. This change of policy was due to various causes. Akbar was associated from boyhood with Hindus and he was married early to Rajput princesses. He saw that there were good men in all religions and therefore came to the conclusion that men were good or bad from causes quite remote from their religious tenets. His chief counsellor in religious matters, Shaik Mubarak, was a pupil of an Afghan Mussulman preacher of the Jaunpur school. By freely mixing with the representatives of various faiths and holding discussions with them on religious topics, Akbar learnt the merits and demerits of each faith and at the same time studied their differences and felt convinced that there was no special saving power in any one religion. He often said: "He is truly a man who makes justice his guide in the path of inquiry and who culls from every creed what reason approves of. Perchance in this way that lock whose key has been lost may be opened." Akbar's religion ultimately took a deistic shape tinged with Hindu and Parsi superstitions. Akbar worshipped the sun. Badayuni says: "The Brahmins now composed a new string of the thousand and one names of the sun. They pretended to consider the emperor an *avatar*, like Rama or Krishna. They cited texts from their old books, prophesying the birth of a king in India, who would be of foreign extraction, but who would protect cows, patronise Brahmins, and govern the world with justice. They showed these prophesies to Akbar and he gave credit to them." Akbar adopted the doctrine of transmigration. Prince Selim was married, in the presence of the emperor and the law officers, to the daughter of Raja Bhagavan Das according to the Hindu ritual. Of the goods with which the ceremonial weighments of the emperor was effected some were distributed among the Brahmins. He adopted the Parsee Naruz (new-year) festival and some twelve others, and enjoined their observance on his provincial officers. He issued several new enactments. A man was restricted to one wife, unless she proved barren. Widows were permitted to marry again. Widows were not to be compelled to perform *sati*, but were not to be prevented from voluntary immolation. In all legal causes between Hindus, a Brahmin was to judge; in those between Mohammedans the Kazi. Cows were ordered to be held sacred and cow dung a purifier. The flesh of cows, buffaloes, horses, camels, and sheep was prohibited, but pork was made lawful. Marriage between first cousins was prohibited. The marriage of boys under sixteen, and girls under fourteen, years of age was prohibited. In all marriages the age of the parties should be verified before the Kotwal. Circumcision was to be deferred till the age of twelve, so that no one is made Mussulman till one could judge for oneself. All persons were declared free to choose their own religion, but, if a Hindu female was induced by affection for a man of the Mussulman persuasion, to join that religion, she might be compelled to abandon it and compulsorily reattached to her original creed. Every one was permitted to erect temples, mosques, churches, or tombs, according to one's own inclination. It cannot be asserted that the zeal of Akbar's Hindu advisers had no hand in some of these enactments, such as the sacredness of the cow and the purificatory efficacy of cow's dung.

Chaitanya was a contemporary of Akbar and in his

teachings we have a striking illustration of the influence of Buddhism on Vaishnavism. Buddhism, though decadent, exercised a considerable influence in Bengal and the neighbouring districts during Chaitanya's time. A biographer of Chaitanya, named Chudamani Dasa, makes Buddhists rejoice at the birth of Chaitanya. One of the great millionaires of Satgao in Chaitanya's time, belonging to the Sonar Bania caste, refused to accept Vaishnavism on the ground that he would not like to be saved, while the whole world round him was plunged in misery, a Buddhist sentiment absolutely unknown to Hinduism. Chaitanya was born at Navadvipa or Nadia, where in Samskrit Tols the Hindu pandits continued the good work which was carried on at Nalanda and later at Vikrama Sila by the Buddhist monks. Chaitanya acquired a great reputation as a scholar and established a Tol of his own. An atmosphere of scepticism, due to the influence of Buddhism, pervaded the Tols of Nadia. Chaitanya went on a pilgrimage to Gaya, and at the temple of the feet of Vishnu (*Vishnupad*) came in contact with a venerable Vaishnava who initiated him into the *bhakti* cult. He taught that even the out-caste was superior to the most learned Brahmin if he were pious and had the love of God. It is believed that with a view to win over those who had been attracted by the teaching of Buddhism, as well as those to whom the grosser forms of the popular Hinduism were repellant, Chaitanya laid stress on the doctrine of *ahimsa*, the duty of avoiding by all means injury to any living thing, and enjoined the equality of all men as a weapon against the established social order, while at the same time it served as an attractive and persuasive appeal to the middle and lower classes, from whom Chaitanya's followers were mainly recruited. A few Mohammedans also became converts to his faith. But the Brahmins stood aloof, as the acceptance of his doctrines implied the surrender of their ancient privileges. Chaitanya was largely influenced by the practices obtaining at the temple of Jagannath at Puri, where he died. A Brahmin sneers at the reforms of the followers of Chaitanya as follows: "In the name of Chaitanya they call upon thirty six castes to dine in the same place; and the pariah, washerman, the oilman and kotal, all sit down cheerfully to dinner without observing any distinction of castes. They pay one rupee and four annas to a Vaishnava priest and marry a widow with children; and in their community a Mohammedan enjoys precedence, in regard to caste being regarded as *kulin*". No wonder that a great number of people who, by adhering to Buddhism, lost all social prestige and were treated as outcastes, readily responded to the brotherly call of the Vaishnavas and gathered under the flag of equality of Nityananda, the great apostle of Chaitanyism in Bengal in the sixteenth century.

In another respect also Buddhism affected the Vishnavite movement in Bengal. The dominant note of Buddhism is the idea of a higher life inspired by a keen sense of morality coupled with introspection. Buddhism lays great stress on chastity. Chastity may be defined as the control of oneself in sexual matters. The sexual function is natural and its normal discharge can not be immoral. The sexual act is not only agreeable to the individual but often necessary for the fulness of one's physical health. It is indispensible to the perpetuation of life. Strict abstinence will involve not only abstinence from all sexual intercourse, but also freedom from sexual perversities, auto-erotic experiences, and indulgence in erotic imaginations, and voluptuous reveries. The will and earnestness necessary for perfect continence can not be presumed to exist in all individuals. Modern psychology declares that the psychic sex nature embodies instincts and wishes which if suppressed in certain ways may express themselves in abnormal ways injurious to the individual and society. No wonder that later Buddhist books declare that salvation is not possible without the cooperation of woman (*strivyatirekena*). Man and woman must fulfil their common destiny as joint partners in a joyful aim at a higher intellectual and ethical life. For such a partnership woman must be morally, civilly, economically, politically free and the equal of man. Love can not reach a high stage of perfection, if it is not free love. Some such ideas coupled with mysticism gave birth to the Vajrayana, and later, the Sahajaya forms of Buddhism in Bengal. The lovers are expected to be both pure in heart and immaculate in morals. But every one knows how difficult it is to control the surging passion of love and remain immaculate. In a society free from caste exclusiveness and stringent marriage laws free love is possible. During the Buddhist times *pratiloma* marriages, highly condemned by Hindu law-givers, were greatly in vogue. Hinduism could not tolerate such freedom, for it would wreck its whole fabric. The revivalists of Hinduism therefore classified into a number of sub-castes those who were born of *pratiloma* marriages and shut the portals of Hindu society against new comers by laying down hard-and-fast rules as to intermarriage and interdining. Human nature being the same everywhere, stringent social rules can not be effective in overcoming the charms of free love. The greater the obstacles to free union, the stronger the impulse which tries to find expression in personal choice. In Hindu society women are entirely cut off from men and live either as drudges or as dependent articles of luxury; husbands and wives have often to be bought; and a mute pair join hands without knowing each other. The husband has a jealous sense of ownership of the wife. The ancient custom of lending the wife to a guest, said to have been abolished by Svetaketu, is also a manifestation of this sense of ownership. Adultery is an offence against property, being the illegitimate appropriation of the exclusive claims of the husband on the wife. As Manu puts it, "seed must not be sown by any man on that which belongs to another." The immolation of a widow with her dead husband and the prohibition of the remarriage of a widow are also the obvious results of the jealousy of proprietorship. Child marriage is evidently a safe mode of obtaining a proprietory right over a woman before she is able to judge for herself. In such a society there can be few opportunities for the meeting of men and women. Still, suppressed passion will find new resources for satisfying itself. In Vaishnavite religious circles a new form of *bhakti* was evolved. Bhakti became an emotional condition in which the devotee glows with the same uncontrollable desire to meet the deity adored as a lover does for his love, laughs and weeps by turns, and even falls into long trances of unconsciousness. There can be no doubt that the divine raptures experienced in these trances are due to the unconscious activity of some of the organs of sexual life. The literature of this *bhakti* abounds in songs and lyrics which have a distinct erotic tinge. Some Puranas have not failed to meet this human weakness. In their zeal for devotion to gods they go so far as to declare that a single utterance of the name of Krishna, Rama, or Siva is enough to wash off many a sin. Thus arose among certain sects the rites of promiscuity and the condonation of adultery. Coupled with the belief in soul and its transmigration this tendency bloomed into Gopis singing, dancing and sporting with Krishna. We may therefore say that the doctrines of the later Buddhists still linger in the Sahaja Siddhi of the Vaishnavas all over India.

The Mohammedan conquest of Bengal led to the destruction of the two great centres of Buddhistic learning, Odantapura and Vikrama-Sila. The Buddhist teachers, who were not killed, fled to other countries. Some of the surviving ministers of Buddhism migrated to Orissa (Utkala) and there built new monasteries which helped to arrest the tide of extinction which threatened to engulf Buddhism. Buddhism was the prevailing religion of Orissa till the time of Raja Prataparudra of Utkala in the sixteenth century. Owing to the persecution of the Buddhists by Purushottama and his successor Prataparudra, a large majority of them embraced the Vaishnavism of Chaitanya. But some of their leaders only professed outwardly the Vaishnavite faith, and were in their heart of hearts sincere and staunch votaries of the Buddha. There are six great devotees (*dasas*) who are generally regarded as the principal Vaishnava poets of Utkala, their works being regarded as the principal Vaishnava literature of the country. When we scrutinise these works, we find that their authors were sincere Buddhists who, for fear of persecution by the Brahmins and their royal patrons, found it necessary to conceal their Buddhism under the guise of Vaishnavism. One of these six *dasas*, Achyutananda, says in his *Sunya Samhita*: "It is desirable in the Kaliyuga that the followers of Buddha should be disguised." Almost all the ancient poets of Orissa refer to Jagannatha or the *Daru-Brahma* as being one and the same with the incarnation of Buddha. Jagannatha Dasa, one of the above six, says in his *Bhagavatha*: "Coming down to the world as the all-wise Buddha the Lord will diffuse knowledge, give up the religion inculcated in the Vedas and promulgate the doctrine of *nirguna*. None will then worship *maya* again. And at this time, all the different castes will again sit together when partaking of boiled rice." So also says Chaitanya Dasa, another of these six, in his *Nirguna Mahatmya*, after finding fault with all the other incarnations of Vishnu, that the Buddha is pure and stainless, that "holding works, religious practices, sacrifices, austerities, religious vows, *tarpanas*, etc., equally useless with respect to the fruits they are expected to yield, he followed simply the sequence of actions, accepting their results unaffected in the least." Twenty two years after the death of Prataparudra Mukunda Deva (1551) ascended the throne. He was a zealous supporter of Buddhism. It is evident from the *Yasomati Malika* of the *Mahima Dharma* sect that Jagannatha, the deity of Puri, passed for Buddha till the first year of the reign of this king. With the close of his reign the Buddhists began to pass their lives in concealment and seclusion. It is believed that on the close of the reign of Mukunda Deva a massive wall was built up to obstruct the view from the outside of the gigantic statue of Buddha discovered behind what now passes for the temple of Surya Narayana within the very precincts of the temple of Jagannatha. The existence of this statue within the temple and its obstruction from outside view by a wall bespeaks the past history of the temple.

The son and grandson of Akbar were too indifferent to religion and too dependent upon their Rajput kinsmen to meddle with the religion of the Hindus. But Aurangazib, though humane by nature, was a rigid puritanical Muslim, who was sternly repressive of himself as of the people around him. In his daily life he observed not only the minute details of Muslim ritual but also practised an extreme austerity. He ate no meat, drank only water, kept all the vigils and fasts, passed whole nights in prayer and in reading the Quran in the mosque, gave alms profusely, and was most simple in dress and manners. He detested the dancing of nautch girls, loud conversation and all laxity of morals. He ordered that public women must marry or clear out of the realm. In strict accordance with Mohammed's precept that every Muslim should practice a trade he made skull caps. With the rigid puritanism of a Muslim was coupled an indomitable will, a cool courage, and a self-sacrificing sincerity, which prepared him to stake his throne for the sake of his faith. For any doctrine which pretends to absolute certitude established by faith intolerance—doctrinally always, practically when circumstances permit it—is a vital condition. How could such a rigid Muslim as Aurangazib tolerate idolatrous practices? He therefore ordered the destruction of Hindu temples. The governors of provinces were strictly enjoined to put a complete stop to the teaching and practising of idolatrous forms of worship. The destruction of the temple of Adi Visvesvara at Benares and the erection of a stately mosque thereon began the storm. The Hindu devotees, called Satnamis (adorers of the true name) rebelled, but the rebellion was sternly suppressed. The imposition of the intolerable *jizya* or poll-tax on all non-Muslims turned the whole Hindu population against Aurangazib. An interference with the infant princes of Marwar led to the loss of Rajput loyalty. Through the energy of Sivaji a new Hindu power came into existence. The Brahmins hailed Sivaji as the champion of Hinduism (*go brahman pratipalak*). Though he belonged to the Sudra stock, the Brahmins, though they had declared that Kshatriyas had been extirpated long ago, fabricated for Sivaji a Kshatriya pedigree and invested him with the sacred thread, the distinctive badge of the twice-born caste. But in their usual way the Brahmins did not teach him the true *mantras* or rules of life of the twice-born so that in this respect he might not be put on a level with them. All the same Sivaji lavished enormous sums of money on the Brahmins and posed as their *chatrapati*. Sivaji "wished to save from Moghul attack a Hindu society, of which ceremonial distinctions and isolation of castes were the very breath of life. He wanted to make this heterogeneous mass triumphant all over India! He wove ropes of sand; he attempted the impossible. It is beyond the power of any man, it is opposed to the divine law of the universe to establish the *swaraj* of such a caste-ridden, isolated, internally-torn sect over a vast continent like India."

While Aurangazib was struggling to restore order, trouble arose in another quarter. By his order Teg Bahadur, the father of Guru Govind Singh, the tenth and last Guru of the Sikhs, was murdered at Delhi. This created in the latter a bitter animosity towards Mohammedans with whom his four predecessors were in conflict. Guru Govind was brought up as a Hindu devotee of the goddess Durga and does not seem to have troubled himself with the teachings of his predecessors. He devoted himself entirely to reorganising the Sikhs on a fighting basis and converted the whole body of Sikhs into an army, named the Khalsa (the pure), and conferred on each member of the body his own name *singh* (lion). Guru Govind also abolished caste distinctions among his followers, and admitted into his army men from all castes.

Had it not been for the Rajputs and the Mahrattas Hinduism would have collapsed during the reign of Aurangazib. Outside of Rajaputana and Maharashtra the amorphous character of Hinduism gave it enough strength to survive the blow inflicted by the Mohammedan invasion. Buddhism collapsed when its monasteries were burnt and its monks were slain. But Hinduism had no centre of religious life, no single administrative body, whose destruction might have caused a general collapse. Its caste organization, its perpetual round of ceremonial observances, which make Hinduism more a social polity than a religion, enabled it to survive. The strength of caste is such that many of the religious reformations in India, which started with the assertion of equality of mankind and the abolition of caste, have in course of time succumbed to the distinctions of caste. The members of the Lingayit sect protest at the present day against all of them being grouped together and demand a differentiation into Brahmins, Kshatriyas, Vaisyas and Sudras. Though Kabir preached against caste, the modern Kabir Panthis prefer that members of unclean castes should join other sects, and should not wear the rosary of wooden beads which mark their own members, and those that claim to belong to the twice-born castes wear the sacred thread of the Hindus. There is a great tendency on the part of the Sikhs to conform to official Hinduism. Among those professing to be followers of Chaitanya, caste has reasserted its sway, and the higher castes maintain their rigid exclusiveness and separation from the lower. Though caste is unknown to the Mohammedan religion, yet it exists in full force amongst many of the Mohammedans of Upper India and in all parts of the country amongst the functional groups that form the lower strata of the community. Mohammedanism, in contact with Buddhism, gave birth to Sufism with its pantheism, its idealism and its universal tolerance. And this in its turn enabled the Mohammedan to meet the animism of the Hindu by the worship of saints, their tombs and relics.

Buddhism still exists in India in various corrupt forms. During the reign of Dharmapala II in the eleventh century Ramai Pandit, Lausena, and others introduced a form of popularised Buddhism under the name of Dharma Thakurapuja for the worship of Dharma, the chief member of the Buddhist *triratna* (Buddha, Dharma, Samgha). To extol the might of Dharma they composed the *Sunya Purana* and the several *Dharmamangalas*. The *Sunya Purana* of Ramai Pandit lays down the rules for Dharma worship. Among these rules one is that Dharma Raj condemns sacrifices. In one passage of this book it is stated that Dharma Raj is held in high veneration in Ceylon and in another we read that Dharma Raj is the Lalita. Avatara, reminding us of the biography in Samskrit of the Buddha known as the *Lalita vistara.* There can therefore be no doubt about the identity of Dharma Thakur with Buddha. In Bengal at the present day there is a very large member of lower class people, who are called Doms. These do not acknowledge the superiority of the Brahmins and are consequently looked down upon by the latter. All their religious ceremonies are performed by pandits of their own class, who are the constituted *purohits* of Dharma. The temples of Dharmaraja, found in large numbers in South India, apparently owe their origin to this form of Buddhism. The priests of these temples are also men of low class. Saraki Tantis, found in the districts of Cuttack, Puri, Bankura, Burdwan, still worship Buddha along with the Brahminic deities. The word *saraki* is Prakrit form of the word *sravaka.* There was a revival of Buddhism in Orissa during the last quarter of the nineteenth century under the name of Mahima Dharma (Alekha Dharma). A man of low class, Bhima Bhoi Arakshitadasa, who earned his livelihood by manual labour, preached his casteless doctrine about Sunya through poetical works and charming hymns. Within a few years he made thousands of followers and his influence became so great that he led the people of about thirty villages upon Puri during the time of its Raja Divyasimha Deva with the express object of making known the real character of Jagannatha as Buddha. The Raja, reinforced by a body of police officers, routed the Mahima-Dharmins, and some of those that were captured were transported on charges of murder by the British government. After this event the followers of this religion, fearing persecution, took refuge in the hills and Gadajats of the forests of Orissa. One of their books, the *Yasomatimalika,* says: "In the Kaliyuga the devotees are passing their lives in disguise, though they have not yet seen the form of the incarnation of the Buddha, in the hope that the *gādi* of the Sunya will be established in the province of Behar and there the Lord Alekha will through his creative power assume the form of a human being in the incarnation for the good of his devotees, who will thus attain emanicipation." It is noteworthy that Buddhism has everywhere and always stood against caste distinctions.

Christianity under the aegis of a Christian government is making rapid progress among the illiterate masses. Though it makes a boast of the fatherhood of God and the brotherhood of man, yet it has not given sufficient strength to its followers to overcome caste prejudices. The Christian Church made no attempt to correct the narrowness of caste prejudice, but accepted the ranks of the Roman empire and the divisions of the feudal system. The Roman Catholic Church in India allows their converts to retain their original caste distinctions. Some Roman Catholic missionaries deliberately accepted the role of *yogi* to make converts. Though the Protestant missionaries forbid caste distinctions, yet they have not wholly succeeded in obliterating these distinctions Says a recent writer in a Christian missionary magazine: "It is an extraordinarily difficult matter, a matter in which we must distinguish between what is ideally right and practically expedient. We ask, why is this? It is not due to the dislike of the clean for the dirty, nor of the cultured for the barbarous. We are forced then to the answer that the reason of the cleavage between black and white is to be found in an instinctive colour prejudice. It is the instinctive antipathy, which explains why quite devout English will not sit down to table with a cleanly well-dressed black man." In aloofness from the moral and spiritual struggle of millions of their fellows these Christian missionaries are no better than Brahmins. Christianity has not been able to prevent Christian nations from exploiting helpless people and setting the world aflame with hate and war. As M. Loisy puts it, Christianity has "passed over the world like a happy dream of immortality without leaving a trace of that law of love which it vaunted as peculiarly its own." Christianity to-day has no moral power left and means little more than hypocritical attachment to puerile dogma. It expects you either to receive some "kingdom of heaven" like a little child or to prostrate your intellect before an infallible authority. It is an anti-intellectual religion and can not shake itself off from the spirit of its founders. It can do nothing with people with any pretentions to culture. Its spread among the ignorant is due to the connection of its missionaries with the ruling class, to their masquerading in the garb of Western civilization, and to the elaborate organizations which employ their influence in many insiduous ways to propagate spiritual slavery and its concommitant political and industrial slavery. Those who boast of the civilizing power of Christianity have only to be reminded of filthy, barbarous and superstitious

Abyssinia where unadulterated pristine Christianity has swayed for centuries without the influence of the Renaissance and the non-Christian thinkers. Christianity plunged Europe for twelve centuries into the appalling misery and ignorance of the Dark Ages. The improved morality of Christian countries goes hand in hand with scientific appliances and democracy. In spite of its modern apologists Christianity is incapable of popularizing the ideas of fraternity and equality. Mohammedanism, which is a mixture of Christianity and Judaism, adapted to the traditions and temperament of the Arabs, is far superior in this respect. The Roman Catholic Church canonised the Buddha under the name of St. Josaphat, which name has been proved to be no other than a corruption of *bodhisattva.* Indian Christianity is gradually taking a Vedantic colouring.

The contact of Hinduism with Christianity and the assimilation of the results of Western thought by educated Hindus have given birth to different reconstructions of Hinduism in order to adapt it to new conditions. The result of one such reconstruction is the *Brahma Samaj* founded by Raja Ram Mohan Rai. Ram Mohan early made the acquaintance of the Christian missionaries at Serampore, and in rendering help in the translation of the New Testament into Bengali he was unable to accept the meaning put by the missionaries on certain passages. However, one of the missionaries took his side and he professed Unitarianism. A Unitarian society was started and worked for several years but without success, as it held its services in English. The failure of this society led to the establishment of a Samaj with services in the vernacular. The congregational worship, common in Mohammedanism and Christianity, was introduced into Hinduism, and the service consisted in the reading of the Upanishads, a sermon, and the singing of hymns. Ram Mohan Rai was also an ardent social reformer, and worked hard against polygamy and for the remarriage of Hindu widows. He was mainly instrumental in inducing Lord Bentinck to put down the inhuman custom of *sati,* the burning of a Hindu widow on the funeral pyre of her husband. Though a man of large sympathies, he was too much of a Hindu to renounce caste. He did not remove the Brahminical sacred thread and when he visited England he took with him a cook to prepare his food in accordance with caste regulations. After his death in Bristol in 1833 the cause steadily decayed, but the liberality of Prince Dwaraka Nath Tagore kept it up.

In 1841 the Samaj received new life by the accession to its ranks of Debendra Nath Tagore and his friends who formed members of the Tathvabodhini Sabha. Unlike Ram Mohan who appealed to the Christian Bible as well as the Hindu Veda, Debendra desired to be wholly a Hindu. In 1846 Debendra declared: "We consider the Vedas, and the Vedas alone, as the standard of our faith." The society thus tended to become a Vedic Samaj and one of its aims was also the arrest of the progress of Christianity which began to make headway through the educational institutions opened by Christian missionaries. But a closer and deeper study of the Vedas led to the abandonment of the Vedas as the standard of the Brahma faith and to the acceptance of nature and intuition as the only sources of the knowledge of God as a personal being with sublime moral attributes, who can be worshipped by all castes and races in spiritual ways. In 1857 Keshab Chandra Sen joined the Samaj and he influenced Debendra to change his Hindu proclivities. Debendra gave up the Brahminical thread and worked out for the use of the Samaj domestic rites freed from Hindu ceremonialism and idolatry. The practice of permitting only Brahmins to lead the services was set aside and Keshab Chandra Sen, though not a Brahmin, was ordained a minister. It was also arranged that no minister should be allowed to wear the sacred thread. Following the example of Keshab some of the members of the Samaj began to give their wives more liberty in defiance of all Hindu custom. Debendra's Hindu temperament inclined him more to the spiritualizing of religion than to changes demanded by the social health of the people. He was therefore against enforcing the regulation about the giving up of the sacred thread by those who led the devotions of the Samaj. This led to a schism and his party left the Samaj.

A new Samaj was founded in 1866 with the distinct motive of rising above the limitations of the Hindu system to a rational faith which would give complete intellectual and social freedom. The service was remodelled. Besides the usual prayer and hymns, it included the reading of passages from the Hindu, Christian, Mohammedan, Zoroastrian and Confucian scriptures which agreed with the principles of Brahmaism. The exceedingly emotional nature of Keshab made prayer one of his joys and necessities. His early Vaishnavite training turned his mind towards *bhakti*, which became the watchword of the new movement. Vaishnavite modes of worship were introduced, the singing of hymns being accompanied by musical instruments. The Vaishnavite *nagarkirtan* or procession through the streets with flags flying and drums beating, with chorus singing and dancing, was bodily taken over. To the two sources of knowledge of God recognised by Debendra's *Adi Samaj* Keshab added a third, namely, God in history speaking through great men. He declared that inspiration (*adesa*) formed a means by which God revealed His will on special occasions though His servants. These ideas appeared to some members of his Samaj to imply a kind of *gurupuja* and autocracy, while they wanted a democratic regime in the Samaj. While Keshab allowed women to be present at services, he was not inclined to give them greater liberty and allow them the benefits of university education. To avoid a breach in the Samaj he laid great stress on *vairagya* or separation from the things of this world. But a flagrant violation of his own principles against child-marriage and idolatrous ceremonies in giving away his minor daughter in marriage to a minor Hindu prince forced a large number of men of character and influence to leave Keshab and form a third Samaj, consisting wholly of those who were willing to renounce caste and give up Hindu rites in their domestic occurrences.

The *Adi Samaj* of Debendra, owing to its endeavour to remain within the caste system, lost its individuality and withered. Keshab's fantastic *New Dispensation* has a comparatively small following. The *Satharana Samaj*, the third Samaj, stands completely outside the caste system and scrupulously avoids every contact with Hindu ritualism and worship. The *Prarthana Samajes* of Western India resemble the *Sadharana Samaj*, but they have not completely renounced the caste system. The census report of 1900 says: "Many who are really Brahmos, other than those of the *Sadharana Brahma Samaj* sect, prefer to describe themselves as Hindus."

An indigenous reforming religious movement, very popular in Northern India at the present day, is the *Arya Samaj* founded by Swami Dayanand Saraswati. In his wanderings through British India Dayanand was impressed deeply by railways, canals, telegraph wires, steam engines and other inventions of modern science. But his mind was saturated with the spirit of India as embodied in the Vedas, the Sutras and the epics. When he compared the indigenous religion of India, namely, Hinduism, with the religions of foreign origin, namely, Islam and Christianity, he found the former to consist of a vast congeries of faiths, ranging from the *Advaita Vedanta* of Samkara to the crudest and grossest superstitions, the whole being held together in a kind of superficial unity by the hierarchical organization of caste. He desired to effect a synthesis between the past culture of India and the science of the West. He found the method of doing this in the assumption that the Vedas as the revealed word of God must contain the basic principles of all the sciences. On this assumption every scientific discovery and invention must be found expressed, germinally at least, in the Vedas. The East was endowed with the faculty of *seeing* and to the West was attributed the faculty of doing or realizing. Hence the West, in realizing the principles laid down in the Vedas, was only unconsciously following the Vedic religion. Not only were the Vedas the revealed source of all the sciences, but they also formed the fountain head of religion, as they formed a primitive revelation given once for all to mankind. Thus by an audacious and uncritical assumption has Dayanand attempted to solve the age-long conflict between religion and science. The fundamental principle of the Arya Samaj is the eternity of God, soul, and matter; *karma* is inexorable, and by means of transmigration each individual soul attains salvation by its own effort. God merely presides over the inexorable process of transmigration and Karma. The Arya Samaj has rejected idolatry, superstitions ceremonies, and pantheism with its doctrines of illusion and absorption. It is fighting vigorously against caste, child marriage and intemperance and showing a praiseworthy enthusiasm for education and social reform. By its pretentious claim that the Vedas are the original source of all the sciences and religions of the world it is ministering to the patriotic spirit of the Hindus. "The person who oppugns the Vedas and the works written by great sages in consonance with the Vedas should be driven away as an atheist from the company of the virtuous—tribe, society and country." It keeps in close touch with Hinduism through the fact of many of its members not having broken caste. It employs preaching, education, tract distribution, newspapers and all other methods of work current among various missionary bodies all over the world. Unlike the Brahma Samaj it has adopted towards Christianity and Mohammedanism an attitude of hostility rather than of eclecticism. Swaraj is declared to be essential to its propagation. "Swaraj is as essential for Vedas as air for men. It is impossible to spread the Vedas without Swaraj (Vedic *chakravartiraj*). No religion has spread without political power; Swaraj is therefore an inevitable and unshakable means of propagating the Vedic religion". No wonder that it has the support of advanced political parties in Northern India.

Two other movements, which have come into being in recent years in support of Hinduism, are more apologetic than reformatory. They are not very enthusiastic about social reform. Both of them are staunch advocates of the doctrines of Karma and transmigration. They give succour to the devout polytheist who is fondly attached to rites and customs. They ask the modern educated Hindu not to reject and despise the religion of the multitude, but to practise diligently the ceremonies of their fathers. They do not work energetically towards the elevation of women, whose ignorance forms the prop of Hinduism. They silently accept the system of caste and even try to defend it, because caste as an organised social system gives Hinduism strength to resist assaults upon the rationality or the truth of its doctrinal tenets. These two movements may be described as expressions of the wily nonchalance of the Hindu towards his festering political humiliation. One of these two movements is the new development of Vedanta taught by Sri Ramakrishna Paramahamsa and expounded by his disciple Swami Vivekananda; the other may be called "theosophical" Hinduism.

The message of Ramakrishna Paramahamsa as expounded by Swami Vivekananda is as follows: "Do not care for doctrines, do not care for dogmas, or sects, or churches, or temples; they count for little compared with the essence of existence in each man, which is spirituality, and the more that is developed in a man, the more powerful he is for good." He repudiates the characterization of Hinduism as polytheism. "In every temple, if one stands by and listens, one will find the worshippers apply all the attributes of God —including omnipresence—to the images. This is not polytheism." He does not repudiate idolatry, but offers an explanation in support of it. The devout worshipper before an idol "recognises in it a necessary stage of his life. The child is the father of the man. Would it be right for the old man to say that childhood is a sin or youth a sin? Nor is image worship compulsory in India." The ideal religion is what the Hindus call Yoga, "union between God and man, union between the lower self and the higher self. To the worker it is union between man and the whole of humanity; to the mystic, between the lower and the higher self; to the lover union between him and the God of love; and to the philosopher it is union in all existence." Because Hindu mythology has a "theory of cycles that all progression is in the form of waves," so it is consistent with the principle of evolution. The absence of any special founder in Vedanta is taken as giving it a claim for universal acceptance. The teaching of the Vedanta is said to be "in entire harmony with the results which have been attained by the modern scientific investigations of external nature." The attitude of this renovated Vedantism towards social reform is clear from the following utterance of its exponent: "Most of our modern reform movements have been inconsiderate imitations of Western means and methods of work, and that surely will not do for India." Thus there is no repudiation of caste, child-marriage and other baneful social practices.

Theosophical Hinduism originated in the Central Hindu College under the aegis of Mrs. Annie Besant. Hinduism, under the name of *sanatanadharma* (eternal religion), is claimed to be the oldest of the world religions, eternal because the truths taught by it are eternal. It depends upon the four Vedas and other scriptures written by *rishis*, such as the *Laws of Manu*, the *Puranas*, the *Mahabharata* and the *Ramayana*. There is one boundless eternal being, Brahmam, or Parabrahmam, who is known only when revealed as Isvara, "the Lord, the loving Father of all the worlds, and of the creatures which live in them." He helps us to know him "by taking different forms, each of which shows us a little portion of Him." These forms are the three great *devas*—Brahma, Vishnu and Siva. He also manifests himself in the form of *devas* and *devis*—Vayu (wind); Agni (fire); Varuna (water); Kubera; and so forth. Besides these are Sarasvati and Ganesa, "who will help us to learn, if we ask them." God lives in us, in our hearts, in our inner self. He shines out on us when we are loving and pure, and is clouded when we are crude or unclean. "He lives in all animals, and even in plants and stones. He is everywhere, helping every one and everything, and we can not do harm to any without hurting Him." He shows himself in incarnations (*avatara*), and He has done so specially in the manifestations of Vishnu. Man is both spirit (*jiva*) and body. As the *jiva* is a portion of Isvara it can not die; at death *jiva* leaves the body behind 'like a worn out cloth' and goes into the other world dressed in other bodies. Then it puts off another of these and "goes on to *svarga*, and is very happy there, till the *svarga* body is also worn out." In the next world a very good person is happy, "but does not stay long"; but a bad person is very unhappy, suffers a great deal, and has to stay there a long time. When the *svarga* body is burnt out, the *jiva*, helped by the *devas*, begins to make some new bodies for himself, as a man might get new clothes, then it comes back to the earth and is born in a new baby body. The conditions of its new birth are determined by its desires, thoughts and actions in its previous lives, according to the law of Karma. All Hindu religious rites and practices are defended. The *mantra* is "a succession of sounds in a definite order, arranged so as to bring us help and protection from Isvara, or from some *deva* or *devi*." The order of sounds is important because "if notes are played in a particular order, we have a tune; if the order is changed, the tune is spoiled." If a *mantra* be translated into another language, it loses its use, because a non-Indian tune can not be effectively played on an Indian musical instrument, as the latter has not all the notes that the Indian one has. Sacraments (*samskara*) are "ceremonies performed at particular times during life to make the bodies more useful to the *jiva*." The *sraddha* helps the *jiva* "to pass quickly through the world into which he goes at death, and to reach the happy world of *svarga* much sooner than he would do if he were left to himself." It is evident that this movement is strongly apologetic and designed to defend every thing in Hinduism on the basis of what the "theosophist" calls "occult" science.

The British administration of India has in no way tended to weaken the power of caste. The British Government does not profess to modify the civilization of India by spreading Western culture. Its primary object is to secure advantages for Britain by assuring to the Indians security and peace. Being the lineal descendant of a mercantile company, the British Government of India possesses many of the traits of its progenitor. Its home is not India but England. Britain does not retain India in the interests of its people but for its own prestige among the nations of the world. For the exploitation of the country and the maintenance of peace the applications of science have been introduced but their introduction has in no way brought about the removal of caste prejudices. As Risley points out in his *People of India*, "in late years the strength of the Hinduizing movement has been greatly augmented by the improvement of communications. People travel more, pilgrimages can be easily made, and the influence of the orthodox section of society is thus more widely diffused. Railways, in particular, which are sometimes a solvent for caste prejudices, have in fact enormously extended the area within which these prejudices reign supreme." Those castes which possess claims to social eminence are most tenacious in asserting and maintaining them. Those below the "twice born" classes are endeavouring to claim equality with them. Even the untouchable despised classes are quite prepared to go into the caste system if its doors would be opened to them. The prestige of the Brahmin still continues to be the centre of magnetization of the divided Hindu society. Though there is in some parts of India much irritation between the secularised Brahmin and the non-Brahmin Hindu for the former's possession of many of the loaves and fishes and even crumbs of Government service, yet the latter has not budged an inch to throw off the heavy shackles which have been inflicted on him for centuries by the caste system. Even in the matter of office-climbing all non-Brahmin Hindus are not of one mind. The division of Hindu society into mutually exclusive compartments has made it incapable of coalescing for active resistance. The subtle political wisdom of the Anglo-Indian officials has not failed to perceive in the caste system a reason for the immobility of Hindu society and an advantage for bringing people to obedience and therefore for ruling the country. As has been remarked by many an English statesman, the secret of Britain's political position in India is in the diversity of creed, race and caste existing side by side. While the Brahminic State was the embodiment of principles and methods based on caste differences, racial discrimination marks British rule in India. Further racial preference characterises British administration everywhere. In the British Empire Canada, South Africa, Australia and New Zealand are entirely independent and in a position to secede at any moment, but Ireland, Egypt, India are retained by the sword and not allowed to govern themselves.

Though under the constitutional British Government there is much individual freedom, the laws are not such as to facilitate intermarriage and bring about the peaceful amalgamation of castes and creeds. Nor has any attempt been made to provide for the young that kind of education which would help to prepare them to form independent judgments and eventually break up the stagnation of the masses of the people. Since the Crown took the government over from the Company, the declared policy is the preparation of the people of India for responsible self-government. But no attempt has been made by the Government to dot the country with those school houses which are the indispensable preliminary to a new social and political order. More money has been spent on the police, the magistracy, the C. I. D., the secret spy system, and the military organization than on education. The organization of services in India on British standards and the undue gap at the top between the emoluments of office and the standards of life cause such a great strain on the finances of the country as to lead one to doubt the possibility of any education of the masses under the present methods. Within fifty years Japan claims to have emerged from "a primitive and purely oriental civilization into a progressive community possessing all the equipment, technical knowledge and resources of a modern State." In the Phillipines in a little more than twenty years under the government of the United States seventy per cent of the population above ten years can read and write. But under the British administration of India for a period of more than one hundred and fifty years only about ten per cent among men and one per cent among women are able to read and write. Even the little education that has been given is wrongly conceived and forms just the minimum required for conducting a foreign government. Education has been imparted with a view to furnish men for the various branches of the Government service. It has made young men look to the State to provide and administer all the necessary services, to exalt clerkship and despise craftmanship. It has brought into existence a large number of office-seekers and a superfluity of adepts in the art of making black look white, but not capable of increasing the country's wealth. The baneful result is that the percentage of population enjoying elementary education is the lowest in any country, while the percentage of males enjoying university education is little below that of England. This anomaly has led to the transference of power into the hands of a class who are using that power in their own interests. The aristocracy of office everywhere endeavours to monopolize the State-machine. Those who possess political power are liable to the temptation of using it for personal or sectional ends, and office often comes to be looked upon as affording opportunity for the accumulation of spoil rather than an occasion for service to the people. Political philosophy has apparently no other function than to supply weapons to the contending parties in the never-ending but ever shifting struggle for power. What could political reform avail in the absence of that mass education on which alone might be based the systematic economic and social reforms so necessary to improve the condition of man? Political rights, however broadly framed they may be, can not elevate people individually low-minded. "It is not by setting up polling booths, but by setting up schools and making literature and knowledge and news universally accessible that the way is opened from servitude and confusion to that willing cooperative State which is the modern ideal." The foundation of society is mutual co-operation, which can be brought about only by an educational process, that will destroy the caste-spirit and the savage egoism that produces in the white man an air of arrogance towards his darker brother. In the world of to-day committed necessarily and rightly to majority rule, our only hope lies in education, in the inculcation of social responsibility, in the development of personality. Without a system of education equally accessible to all there can be no complete and genuine democratization of the State.

The loud cry in the country for national education is indicative more of a dissatisfaction with the British Government than of any definite and positive ideas about the educational needs of the people. The political despair of an emasculated people and the material misery of an impoverished country have engendered the idea of reversion to the practices of a pre-mechanistic age as well as the cry for a meaningless national education. The factors of nationality are the belief in a common origin; the possession of a common language and literature; the pride that is felt in common historic traditions, in the memories of a common political history and of common struggles against foreign foes; community of religion; and community of social customs. To the motley peoples of India not one of these can be regarded as rigorously applicable. No doubt the British administration has brought the inhabitants of a very large portion of India under one government. But that cannot be said to constitute the Indians into a nation. Political allegiance to one government and submission to one law are the characteristics of a State. But State and nation are two notions fundamentally different. The idea of a State has a politico-legal significance and implies merely the union of a portion of mankind into one body politic. On the other hand the idea of a nation involves the oneness of culture and implies the binding together of a similar portion of mankind by other than mere political ties. Nationality does not depend upon but trancends political-allegiance, religious belief and economic interest. Nationality is a form of consciousness of kind which binds men together irrespective of their political allegiance, religious beliefs and economic interests. As a French writer recently put it, "a nationality is neither a territory, nor a race, nor a language, nor a history; it is a will to unite in the present and to endure indefinitely in the future." In other words a nation is animated by a common purpose to be something distinct and to preserve its identity. Responsible self-government seems to be the only common aim actuating the thinking sections of the heterogeneous peoples of India. The only means of achieving this end is education. All education must aim at bringing about the best possible conditions on this planet. Every living healthy system of education must have behind it a social ideal. An educational system worthy of the name must give to every child a chance of growing up into a good and healthy man or woman, fully developed in mind and body. It is the main business of all education to free the mind from shackles and kindle the undying fire of liberty, and it is the subordinate business of special training to train young people to realise their central purpose in a particular form of service to their fellows. However necessary specialization may be, education must fit every man to maintain his human dignity. Education must stand for liberty, the widest possible individual freedom of thought and action. It must wean the mind from the supernatural, to which it turns for the explanation of what it does not understand. It must dispel the fear of invisible powers and guide man from intellectual darkness to light. It must be the great instrument of social change. It must destroy the fissiparous caste and bring about corporate life, corporate growth and corporate self-respect which are so essential to the development of nationality. In a country where a group of men has tricked or forced the rest into believing that the knowledge of truth is open to that group alone on account of special qualifications given to it by birth, the education of the masses is of greater importance than government. Further, in principle the State exists for man, and not man for the State. It is the business of government to provide the conditions of peace, security and freedom in which progress can take place. The world is moved by ideas. If these ideas are in harmony with the striving exurgent world-forces, they are vital and will serve to elevate the type of man. But if they are imposed by men who seek wealth and luxury, economic domination, royal trappings, or priestly authority, they generate their own toxins and serve to degenerate the type of man. "The true view of the universe must be opened to the population of India, even though it should seem to blot out and cancel all the conceptions in which they lived for three thousand years. Such is the awful Nemesis of a system which arrests change too long and too successfully!"

The so-called nationalists of a nationless India boast that the social system of India was perfected thousands of years ago and console themselves by attributing all their miseries to the foreign invasions. But they forget that these invasions have been possible only through the emasculation wrought by spiritual and social slavery. Freedom stands on personality, and personality is bound up with control of the conditions of one's work, so that one may express himself in his product. There is no need for freedom in a society in which a few men decide everything for all the rest. When caste and status delimit life, men are driven to be either fools or hypocrites. No democracy can be built on restrictions which hinder individual liberty and free association. No democracy can grow in a social environment in which the distinction of inferiors and superiors forms an essential and permanent idea. As Mr. Rabindranath Tagore puts it, "the social habit of mind which impels us to make the life of our fellow beings a burden to them when they differ from us even in such a thing as choice of food, is sure to persist in our political organization and result in creating engines of coercion to crush every rational difference which is the sign of life." The ultimate appeal of democracy must always be to men's consciences. But when the conscience is not free, of what avail could the appeal to it be? It is of the essence of caste that, instead of recognising the inviolability of the individual conscience, it constrains and penalises an honest conscience. Democracy is not merely a form of government but a mode of association, of living together. It is what leads to comradeship within one's gates between the servant and the master, the landlord and the tennant, the millionaire and the plough-boy. Democracy represents the spirit of personal equality and fraternity.

As the system of castes is the most vigorous of the causes of social disintegration, it has stood in the way of developing among the Hindus any principle of cohesion or any motive for unity. It has prevented the growth of all idea of patriotism, so that there is not in the Samskrit language nor in the vernaculars of India any old word to represent that sentiment which in other countries has been the incentive for much heroism. Common political life, characteristic of a nation, has been produced in all the recognised nations of the world by the freest intermingling and fusing of the different smaller groups inhabiting a common territory. The modern civilizing tendency towards unity can not be produced by a system whose fundamental principle is isolation. By forbidding intermarriage between the different castes the system of caste has rendered social fusion impossible. Every caste lives for itself with no feelings of commiseration and pity for the sufferings of other castes. This parcelling of the Indian population has produced baneful results. The peculiar peril of a society organised on the basis of caste is anarchy. The dread of anarchy has led to absolute monarchy as the strongest defence against it. The traditional Hindu theory of kingship is rooted in caste and necessarily requires the presence of an absolute ruler, uniting in his own person all legislature for the purpose of enforcing the rules of the various castes. The tiny self-governing republics which existed in Ancient India seem never to have come under the influence of Brahminism. The exclusion of most of the castes from sharing in the political life of the country has left little room for the growth of feelings of common interest and public spirit. The caste system, which is born of the most abject spiritual slavery, has resulted in the political slavery of the Hindus. The Hindus, who have waived their rights in allowing the Brahmins to determine for them the laws under which they should live, have lost their freedom and become servile. The country in which the great right of being one's own master has been systematically suppressed has become a factory of slaves fit only for foreign domination. The vast continent of India with its hundreds of millions of inhabitants has for centuries been the prey of predatory conquerors. Foreigners have been able to ravage the country with fire and sword with the aid of soldiers raised in the country itself. A small body of foreigners suffices to keep in check a host a thousand times stronger than itself. The Hindus have been subject to foreign rule for such a long time that they have become indifferent ~~as to who~~ rules them, whether he be an Englishman sitting in London, or a Frenchman sitting in Paris, or one of themselves sitting in Delhi. With such people what could a mere change in the legislative machine effect? A stroke of the pen can alter an institution, but would it modify the mentality of a people? Priest-ridden, karma-obsessed, maya-enslaved mentality is the source of all the miseries under which the Hindus are groaning. Spiritual slavery, fatalism and superstition have smothered all power of self-reliance and all sense of freedom. Unless a people long for freedom and strenuously work for it, they can not obtain it. A free people will always have the government it deserves.

The spirit of intransigent division which is characteristic of caste has not only rendered impossible all superior organization, but it has also sunk the Hindus into a state of intellectual immobility. As Crozier has pointed out, "where caste is absolute and the barriers that separate class from class are insurmountable, mere rank is everything, and practical intellect, initiative, originality, and enterprise, being alike unavailing to help a man out of the sphere in which he was born, are held in a minimum of regard. The consequence is that these nations have long sunk into a settled and abiding intellectual stagnation." The spirit of caste is inimical not only to the growth of national unity but also to the emanicipation of the individual. It condemns to atrophy the class of men who have become great in the West through their literary and scientific labours. It knows neither the combative eloquence of the public man nor history which reminds people of the great events of the collective life. It ignores those personal effusions which represent the concords and discords of man with himself. Rarely do we come across any literature which is the expression of character freely exercised in choice. In the economic sphere the result has been no better. The multitude of irksome restrictions imposed by the system of castes upon the individual in his public and private life has not only tended to limit production, but it has also destroyed adaptability and rendered inoperative those laws of supply and demand which connect communities with natural resources. A searching examination of every sphere of life forces on all the conclusion that the system of castes, though it may enable by the very order it imposes on a society to emerge out of barbarism, hinders further development by crushing under its own weight the germs of further development into civilization. There can be no civilization without individual freedom. The stability and contentment observed in Hindu society is merely an index of the lack of energy in the people to push themselves forward. A people that rebels is a people that is looking up, that has begun to hope and feel its strength. It is a physical principle that the most stable condition of a system is that in which its potential energy is a minimum. Such a system is incapable of moving itself. This truth is equally applicable to human societies. The most contented and stagnant societies are the most stable. Caste destroys all power of determination *a fronte.* Any person who habitually lives in the notions of caste becomes more or less incapacitated for breadth and delicacy of perception. Class views of any kind inevitably narrow the mind and hinder it from receiving pure truth. The love and pursuit of culture carries each one of us out of his class, to sympathise with the sufferings of all and work for their elevation.

Attempts have been made to buttress caste by scientific props. Caste, it is contended, has an ethnic basis. The Samskrit word for caste being *varna,* which literally means colour, it is urged that between the higher castes, the so-called Aryans, and the lower castes, there is a racial opposition, more or less absolute, arising from a difference in colour. Hundred and fifty years ago John Hunter came to the conclusion that the original colour of man's skin was black, and all the physiological knowledge that has been gathered since his time supports the inference he drew. The microscope reveals no difference between the blond and the black. The human skin, whether it be the skin of the darkest Negro or of the whitest European, always contains only dark pigment. The colour of the white European is not produced by milk or the ichor of the gods of antiquity. The pigment is everywhere the same, and it is always dark. It differs not in quality but only in quantity. In some cases the quantity of pigment is so large that it makes its appearance on the surface, while in other cases it lies hidden in the deeper layers. But the pigment is never absent. The new born babes of all people are of the same colour. The colour of the skin changes with the climate. A large stay in the tropics turns the skin of the European brown, while the skin of the Negro becomes perceptibly bleached by long residence in the temperate zone. The majority of the Brahmins are neither lighter in colour nor better featured than the members of the other castes. As Mr. Nesfield says, they are not distinct in race and blood from the scavengers who sweep the road. Anthropometric measurements show that the cephalic index of the "twice born" does not sensibly differ from the cephalic index of the aborigines, and in regard to nasal index the Kayasths, who, according to the Brahminical theory, are Sudras, take precedence over the Brahmins, and the Chandalas, an impure caste, go before the Rajavansis of royal blood. The whites are not all paragons of beauty and virtue, and the blacks are not all deformed and vicious. The factors, which race-feeling represents to itself as objective, and from which it derives stimulus, are far from being objective in fact. All talk of difference of race is the result of a prejudice, which has only served as a menace to tolerance, to truth, to justice, to righteousness, to honor and international comity.

All attempts to classify mankind into races have proved a signal failure. At best the so-called races of mankind, spoken of by anthropologists and ethnologists, are only hypothetical classifications for convenient description, serving just the same purpose as the theories of physical science. They are, to use an expression of Lamark, mere products of art, the results of mental gymnastics, which have no real counterparts in nature. "Though we flatter," says Emerson, "the self-love of men and nations by the legends of pure races, all our experience is of the gradation and resolution of races and strange resemblances meet us everywhere. It need not puzzle us that Malay and Papuan, Celt and Roman, Saxon and Tartar should mix, when we see the rudiments of tiger and baboon in our human form and know that the barriers of races are not so firm, but that some spray sprinkles us from antediluvian seas." At the present day the unity of the origin of mankind is universally accepted. Differences in the shape of the skull and in the colour of the skin, hair and eyes, are the result of changes produced by environment, migration and miscegenation. The various stocks of man can be derived from a generalised type with primitive characters by differentiation and specialization along different collateral lives in different environments. Man has never differentiated into different species but only into a number of varieties. Varieties can interbreed, while species do not interbreed, or produce offspring which, like mules, are sterile. No classes of human beings are incapable of freely mixing with one another. The so-called great families of peoples, Aryan, Caucasian, Semitic, and so forth, represent unities or similarities of language, from which no inference can be drawn as to a common racial origin. Many branches of these so-called families have mingled again and again. All the great peoples of the ancient and modern world are known to have resulted from intermixture. The difference in racial type, as seen between the white, the yellow, and the black races, is ascribed by some naturalists to alterations in the balance of the various glands of internal secretion. No race of man now in existence can be said to represent a pure unvarying type. Much more than anatomical and physiological considerations, the general similarity of mental and moral endowments and the oneness of the historical development of man in all climes and countries teach us to regard all humanity as a vast brotherhood. In spite of diverse ethnic developments the general history of human culture is the same. Man emerging from savagery passes through barbarism to civilization and ultimately reaches the humanitarian stage. In some cases this development may be arrested. But man everywhere possesses the same innate capacity to learn. All mankind can learn to understand the same language and can adapt itself to cooperation. The mental differences between the different races as between the different classes, is a difference, not of natural endowment, but of opportunity. Human nature being in essence the same everywhere, progress is a matter not connected with the race to which an individual belongs, but with the system of beliefs with which he is indoctrinated. By acquiring scientific knowledge and adopting scientific methods of education, the Japanese have completely changed their mental qualities. Other races can change their mental character as quickly as the Japanese, and history proves this abundantly. A tolerance of racial differences can be achieved only by the categorical denial of conformity. Insistence on a dead conformity is an index of barbarism. To be human is enough. Varieties of character enrich civilization.

The purity of blood for which some men stickle is a pure myth. The *varna sankara* which the orthodox Hindu fears was accomplished centuries ago. "There is hardly a class or caste in India," says D. R. Bhandarkar in his paper on *Foreign Elements in the Hindu population*, "which has not a foreign strain in it. There is an admixture of alien blood not only among the warrior classes—the Rajputs and the Mahrattas—but also amongst the Brahmanas, who are under the happy delusion, that they are free from all foreign element." In the veins of the Brahmins of the present day flows the blood of the Sudras of antiquity, just as in the veins of the white Europeans runs the blood of the Negroes who lived on the continent of Europe during the quaternary period. The infusion of new blood into families and peoples has always been productive of very beneficial results. Dr. Tylor says that he saw the most beautiful women in the world in Tristanda Cunha among the descendants of the whites and the blacks..M. Finot says that the most remarkable examples of longevity are found among the Mulattoes. Whereever crossing has taken place in normal conditions, the types called inferior have improved without causing any degeneracy in the types called superior. The pessimistic assertions of the detractors of crossing are refuted by the fact that peoples who have freely mixed with one another have continuously progressed. Those who are in the vanguard of civilization and progress are those whose blood is most rich in heterogeneous elements. Even when we consider the case of superior individuals in different countries, we are astonished to find that almost all of them are the result of inter-marriages. Havelock Ellis affirms that the best American writers and thinkers are descended from mixed families. On the other hand all attempts to preserve the purity of blood have produced disastrous consequences. History demonstrates how those among the aristocracy of Europe, who have kept aloof from the plebian classes, have either degenerated or died out.

It is not uncommon to find people defending caste from the standpoint of heredity. As Thomas Paine says, "the idea of hereditary legislators is as inconsistent as that of hereditary judges, or hereditary juries, and as absurd as an hereditary mathematician, or an hereditary wise man, and as ridiculous as an hereditary poet-laureate." All that science has to tell us regarding heredity, that is, the individual's contribution to his development, is summed up in the theory of *recapitulation*. Just as the human embryo assumes successive forms which represent the physical evolution of the human species, though with variations, short-cuts, etc., so after birth the individual follows in a rough schematic way the line of mental and social evolution of the race. What the child brings into the world is a psychological organism which reacts reflexly and instinctively to certain stimuli and impulsively and in uncoordinated manner to other stimuli, but in no direction is the child equipped with innate truths or standards. Except in a few cases our knowledge of heredity is very slight and uncertain. The laws of heredity, emphasised by Biometricians and Mendelians are so complex and obscure that we may rely only in a few extreme cases. They may hold good, rigidly or approximately, of colour of eyes or hair, of stature, perhaps even of temperament and energy, but there is grave doubt whether these laws control the intellectual life. Says Bateson in his *Mendel's Principles of Heredity*: "There is as yet nothing in the descent of the higher mental qualities to suggest that they follow any single system of transmission. It is likely that both they and the more marked developments of physical powers result rather from the coincidence of numerous factors than from the possession of any one genetic element." Mental qualities, being the effects of training and surroundings, are merely acquired characters. There is no evidence that they are ever inherited. On the other hand there is overwhelming evidence that they are not inherited. The secret of mental resemblance is not inheritance but association. Example, training, development in a similar environment are sufficient to account for the mental likeness between child and parent Lombroso claims that all those that are respected for morality or intellect were diseased and quite unfit to be progenitors of the race. This view of Lombroso may be false, but it is true that those who possess great powers themselves do not transmit their excellent qualities. The laws of heredity are so complex and so obscure that we have really no science of eugenics in spite of the great noise about it. As Huxley says, "I doubt whether even the keenest judge of character, if he had before him a hundred boys and girls under fourteen, could pick out with the least chance of success, those who should be kept, and those who should be chloroformed, as equally sure to be stupid, idle, or vicious. The 'points' of a good or bad citizen are really far harder to discern than those of a puppy or a short-horn calf." The analogy between the breeding of men and the breeding of dogs or horses is wholly false.

"It needs," says Whetham, "the conjunction of many different factors to produce a man of ability, a woman of beauty and charm. Hence we can not at present at all events, trace the descent of ability, moral character, or beauty in the same precise way as we can follow from generation to generation certain bodily diseases or mental defects." Geniuses do not arise out of any exclusive hierarchy or caste, but appear as capriciously as the wind which bloweth where it listeth, according to laws, if such there be, which have hitherto baffled all eugenists. The ethical culture of an individual depends on voluntary conscious effort towards an end in view and has therefore more to do with education than heredity. The inborn traits of average general development are so mighty that morality can rarely be expected as a natural factor to exhibit greater power than the other factors. Were man left solely to the control of heredity he would exhibit much more the character of an animal than of an ethical being. The most important social traits, those that concern the moral life of mankind, are to be traced, not to a common hereditary constitution, but to a common social environment. A mode of feeling, thought, and conduct, which is widely diffused and stable enough to have become typical, exerts a powerful and almost irresistible influence on the individual. Man is a product not only of nature but also of culture. Imitation stimulates the intellectual and ethical development of the young and enables them to acquire in a few years habits which represent long centuries of endeavour on the part of their ancestors. Human nature is continually changing and is perpetuating its changes by language, arts, laws, institutions, thus creating a new environment which is more important than ancestral inheritance. Even the so-called national characteristics of the people of any country are not innate characters but in the main expressions of different traditions and ideas. The social and physical environment furnishes the whole content of man's rational life. It has been pointed out that in the East African campaign the untrained, almost wild natives showed in the setting and actual construction of light railways and roads a degree of intelligence, enterprise and foresight which would have shamed most men of the British labouring classes. The same writer says that in commercial enterprises the African natives are as "nearly efficient as their more largely trained Hindu competitors, who have the traditions of long generations of artisan forefathers behind them." Each child is a new beginning and the path to virtue is as open to the child of the Pariah as to the child of the Brahmin. *Janmana jayate sudra, karmana jayate dvijah.* Every one born of women is a Sudra, but the practical life of the social environment into which one enters renders one twice-born. Evil habits of sordid surroundings keep flowing on to posterity by home or environmental contagion.

Though we may not call in question the existence of natural inequalities among human beings, yet we can not but admit their fundamental equality when we consider them as rational beings and moral potentialities. The ideal goal of human progress consists in the development and exercise of those capacities which, from the highest ethical standpoint, should be cultivated and employed. This necessitates the existence of a regime in which the criteria of fitness for success will be the possession of absolutely the highest moral qualities. It naturally implies that no one shall find himself born into a social world in which one is to any degree so bound by social requirements which render it impossible for him to develop to the fullest his capacities, to refine to the fullest his desires, and to reap to the fullest the rewards of his individual merit. The impossibility of securing all this under the regime of caste, which relegates certain sections of the community as hopelessly inferior to others, is obvious. Caste pride and class exclusiveness have always stood in the way of good government and the growth of liberty; they have been the curse of the world in the past and will prove her ruin in the future. Social reformers might have laid stress upon contentment in men and stability in institutions, but none of them has desired the establishment of a stereotyped caste system. "If indeed no effort is made," says John Ruskin, "to discover in the course of their early training, for what services the youth of a nation are individually qualified, nor any care taken to place those who have unquestionably proved their fitness for certain functions, in the offices they could best fulfil—then to call the confused wreck of social order and life brought about by malicious confusion and competition an arrangement of Providence, is one of the most insolent and wicked ways in which it is possible to take the name of God in vain." The organic conception of society demands the responsibility of all to each and each to all. In an organism all the members may not be discharging functions of equal value. Still all are regarded as of equal value and are given equal opportunity for development for discharging their functions in the best manner. This does not imply absolute equality but equality of opportunity for self-development and social service. The rejection of the system of hereditary castes is not based upon an abstract assertion of equality, but upon historical facts and scientific interpretations, which refute the utility of such a system. Nature has endowed some men with greater powers and denied them to others. But no human agency should be permitted to aggravate the natural disability and clog the path of progress.

Equality of opportunity means that success shall be determined by talent and energy and not by the accident of birth. The abolition of special privilege, the wider and more equal distribution of wealth, the extension of facilities for education, the increase of inter-communication these are some of the means of affording equality of opportunity. Mere *laissez faire* does not constitute opportunity. Equal opportunity has to be created by annulling the tyranny of circumstance and actively intervening against established injustice. One can not be given opportunity without the acknowledgment of one's worth. Honour and dignity can not be regarded as the exclusive prerogatives of a caste, or class, or race. Self-respect resents arrogance and disparagement and demands fraternity, which implies fair-mindedness, courtesy and the admission of one's own limitations. Without fraternity there can be no fellow-citizenship and fellow-humanity. Fraternal self-respect demands that a man ranks with his fellows, even though he may have achieved glory and distinction. A polity of caste and privilege can never be consistent with social equality. Men may be unequal, but they are all men; they may differ in the degree of their capacity, but they possess capacity of the same type. Reason is the common mark and nobility of all men. What Shylock says of a Jew, can be said of any man: "Hath he not eyes? Hath he not hands, organs, dimensions, senses, affections, passions? fed with the same food, hurt with the same weapons, subject to the same diseases, healed by the same means, warmed and cooled by the same Winter and Summer, as his fellow is?" The possession by all men of similar innate capacity for happiness and misery is the basis for the right of every individual to participate in the control of public policy. Without perfect equality of opportunity for all classes alike, there is no possibility of determining the actual merit of any individual. The broad duty of society is so to arrange its institutions that success is to the best according to the highest human ideal. Without a social order based on the principles of a just and equitable organization the survival of the fittest according to the highest human ideal is not possible. Only out of equal rights and privileges for all will emerge justice, human dignity human solidarity and unity.

Those in power not infrequently think that they are necessarily more capable of development than those whom they regard as their inferiors. Such a proposition is unwarranted by the teachings of science. One well-established fact of evolution is that in the "higher" form of a species there is a tendency to revert to the typical form. Hence it would seem possible that the descendants of those who are now thought low and base might, if time and opportunity were given them, rise to the typical form of the species, and even go beyond it, while it is not impossible that the successors of those who are now regarded as representing a higher type might revert to the typical form of the species, and even degenerate to a lower condition. Of this history furnishes ample proofs. As Nietzsche points out, "the rough energy of the camp, the deep impersonal hatred, the cold-bloodedness of murder with a good conscience, the general ardour of the system in the destruction of the enemy, the proud indifference to great losses to one's own existence and that of one's friends, the hollow, earthquake-like convulsion of the soul, can as forcibly and certainly be communicated to enervated nations" If such differences as exist between the present nations of Europe are the result of a difference in environment and individual variability, and if the relation between the organism and its environment is the ultimate cause of bodily and mental variation, the possibility of progressive development for every people, even the most backward, must be conceded, if only the physical and social conditions of environment can suitably be changed. That among the individuals of all races there are great differences of endowment, capacity and attainment no one will deny. But science, religion and practical politics are agreed in denying the existence of naturally superior races and eternally inferior races. As Dean Inge remarks, the European man has no other superiority to the races which he arrogantly despises than being the fiercest of all beasts of prey equipped with weapons which have made him the lord and the bully of the planet. It is national pride that has been the cause of mutual depreciation between peoples. So long as the most trumpery pin-points of distinction of colour, creed or caste serve as grounds of quarrel, we shall not realise the blessings of a universal peace on earth. Without the political and social equality of all mankind there will be no substantial human advancement.

The theory of the four *varnas* is regarded by some as an ideal to which society ought to conform. Society is for them nothing but the individual written large. The macrocosm of society and the microcosm of the individual must correspond to each other. Just as the body has a head, arms, thighs, and feet, so must society have something corresponding. It must have parts which discharge functions similar to those of the head, arms, thighs, and feet. Society must therefore consist of four classes, devoted respectively to thought fighting, husbandry, and menial service. This is both bad physiology and bad sociology. It is bad physiology because you can not divide the body into self subsistent organs. We work with our whole body, whatever be the kind of work we may do. In all work the whole body, not mere parts, is active. It is bad sociology because you can not make the classes of a society correspond to parts of the body. You can not have one class which merely or even mainly thinks, another which merely works. The great defect of any such conception is that it obscures the true unity of society. For classes so distinguished are related only by way of difference, each fulfilling its nature in contributing superficially distinct functions. Difference of function is indeed essential within a society, but beyond the difference involved in external function there must exist an inward likeness. Society is not simply or primarily the harmony of differences, but the union of likes. The likeness is ultimate. Consequently justice which is a principle of partition, which sees that each par fulfils its function, does not form the deepest ground of social unity. It is only the superficial social relationships, such as the relation of master to servant, employer to employee, buyer to seller, which rest on mere difference, that involve the play of justice. But in a real society the relations of difference that exist imply an identity of nature in the members so related, a relation of likeness on which the relation of difference is founded. Likeness of nature involves likeness of ends and likeness of goods. Without unity underlying differences there can be no division of labour, for division of labour and cooperation are only two aspects of a single fact. The greater the division of labour the more interdependent men become. Therefore you can not split up a society into classes corresponding to distinct and exclusive elements, whether of body or mind. The only inherently evil division of labour is in fact such as would reduce men to the place of parts within a machine, but such a consequence would arise only from a division of labour based on a system of castes for various kinds of work.

The Brahmin frees himself from all this criticism by basing his social philosophy on the belief in a mysterious soul and its occult *karma* and transmigration. For this philosophy the true nature of the individual lies beyond his visible self, and a blind law of justice assigns different duties to individuals according to their birth. All this is flatly opposed to the modern ideal of democracy which demands that men should enjoy equal rights and derive equal benefits from social organization. It is indeed true that aptitude and competence will be the basis of distribution of the necessary activities of society; that classes may arise resting on personal differences, differences of occupation, ability, character, manners. The more classes rest on significant personal differences, the farther are they removed from the evils of a caste system, from the physical repulsion and stagnation it entails. Wealth too is a class-determinant, but being acquirable, alienable, transferable it draws no such permanent lines of cleavage as does birth. When classes rest on intrinsic personal differences and not on mere privilege or status, the interests of the community are best served. But it is an evil to the whole community when some members feel themselves cut off from a share in the complete life or culture of the community. No forms of social service, least of all the highest, should be the privilege of any determined class. All human activity is also social function. It is inhuman and anti-social to condemn arbitrarily and permanently some men to ignoble and repugnant tasks. If a developed society needs base and distasteful tasks to be performed by its members, the only way of doing it is to assign such tasks to all by rotation, so that all members may be assigned equal rank, or to require that every man engaged in mechanical work shall do a portion of his day's work in intellectual employment and that every brain worker shall devote a portion of his day to physical labour. Only thus shall we attain to a condition in which every man shall have, as George Meredith puts it, "a full man's share in what is going on in life."

It is the boast of some that the system of castes has been able to ring out the feud between capital and labour. Perhaps it has done so by rendering it possible for the accident of birth to obliterate the natural capacities of the children of the unfortunate Sudra. The position of the Sudra in the caste system, as laid down in the Shastras, is that of a serf, who is beyond the pale of instruction. This serfdom is the logical consequence of the belief in souls and their transmigration. Says Manu: "If any of the four classes omit without urgent necessity the performance of their several duties, they shall migrate into sinful bodies and become slaves to their foes." The caste system has certainly made India a pleasant spot for the Brahmin to live in among a caste-ridden people, but only at the cost of horrible suffering and destitution for the depressed classes. The Brahmin has turned the majority of Hindus into hewers of wood and drawers of water, depressed intellectually and socially. If the inevitable result of the capitalistic system is seen in the slums of the great cities of the modern world, the squalid disease-striken *paracheries* all over India are the baneful effect of the system of castes. In what way has caste furthered the common weal? Has it brought about a proper distribution of the means of ordinary welfare and comfort? Has it secured for every caste-observing man what is necessary to make life tolerable and give him the blessings of culture? Has caste impelled individuals to associate their labour for the common welfare of all? Has caste tended towards the collaboration and cooperation of all classes for the general progress of all? Has caste put an end to competition and the spoliation of others? While it is necessary that the work done should furnish to the worker not only a wage or salary sufficient to sustain him in the best possible performance of his work, it should also be the means of his intellectual, volitional and aesthetic development But the spirit of caste has invested certain kinds of work with an unnatural odium. While the social impulse belongs to the very fundamental nature of man, caste has tended to breed repulsion between men and to manufacture, as Rabindranath says, a 'magnificent cage of countless compartments." This mutual repulsion between castes has made it impossible even for all the workers in a factory to combine for improving their status. No plan of organization which requires the subordination of many can tend to the development of all its members. A cohesion through the assent and devotion of every member of society is necessary for every individual to regard himself as a public functionary working for the benefit of society. The only system that makes possible the ideal of cohesion compatible with liberty is cooperation, which the spirit of caste tends to destroy. Only through the collaboration of all classes can the general welfare be assured, which would guarantee to every one that minimum of comfort that would give him a chance to be moral and human. Without the acceptance of joint responsibility both by the labourer and the capitalist for the efficient conduct of industry no genuine improvement will occur. This means that labour must have a share in the management of industry, the capitalist must not maintain his emphasis only on profits, and labour its emphasis only on wages and short hours. If labour as a class is ever to rise from the relative misery and poverty of its surroundings, the energy drained away in luxuries and in harmful or unnecessary products must be turned to the production of more of the right kind of stuff—more houses, more food stuffs, more clothing, more schools. Production measured either in money or tons of goods has easily increased, but the production of necessary, well-made, consumable goods, and their distribution among individuals has shown but a slight improvement, and it is only the latter that is of importance to the majority of mankind. Forces on forces are created, new machinery continually devised, new means of communication introduced, but the common weal has not been furthered. Want and misery are the lot of the majority; they live by fraud, chicanery, or servile labour. Seven tenths of the wealth of the world as well as the control of the means of production are in the hands of a few. Men are under the delusion that the spoliation of others and the transformation of themselves into parasites increases their welfare. The competitive organization of society fosters the worst elements in human nature and is not favorable to the cultivation of the virtues required in the love and service of humanity.

Some see an analogy between the system of caste and the scheme proposed by Plato in his *Republic* to regenerate mankind. Plato's scheme for the reconstitution of society was due to his distress at the corruption of the higher classes, on whom rested in his opinion the salvation of the State. His method of logical definition and classification led him to the conclusion that the collective action of men was possible only through a division of labour. From this he argued that in the interest of the whole community every individual ought to be restricted to a single occupation. Hence the industrial classes, who form the bulk of the population, should be excluded from political power as well as military service. Though each profession must be exercised by men trained for it, yet mercenary fighters might employ their power either to oppress and plunder defenceless citizens or to establish a military despotism. Though only men fitted by special training should discharge the functions of government, yet a privileged class might be tempted by the abuse of their position to fill their pockets and gratify their passions. To provide against these dangers and to make them better attend to their duties the rulers and the defenders of the state ought not to possess any property of their own, but should subsist on the labour of the industrial classes. All private interests should be eliminated from their lives. Marriage and domesticity should be abolished, although they might procreate children, who would be the property of the State. Women who produced children for these ruling and military men should have no home employments. They should pass through the same bodily and mental training, be enrolled in the army and discharge, when fitted, the highest political functions. "For Plato the civic ideal is always a united, firmly organised group, the members of which live, as far as possible, a common life, educated from the cradle in common nurseries and schools, eating and drinking at common tables, exercising in common, and having, as far as may be common objects of joy and grief on all occasions of life. The "enemy" is excessive individualism, the pursuitof private well-being, exclusive power, exclusive wealth, exclusive pleasures, whether such individualism assumes the collective form which pursues the exclusive interest of a specially favoured group, such as an industrial class, a political faction, or an aristocratic club, or assumes the more extreme form which produces the superman or tyrant." To the popular ideal of the unconstitutional despot, Plato opposes his ideal of a philosopher-king. The reason for this is that he regards the life of philosophic contemplation as beyond criticism. But society can not allow its finest intellects to withdraw completely from the pressing problems of the community. Hence men and women with the aptitude and training for the life of philosophic coutemplation must at frequent intervals return to the arena of practical life and undertake the task of political administration, not as an object of keen competition but as a social duty, as a form of social service. This short account is enough to show how far Plato's scheme of regeneration of mankind is from the system of castes. As has already been pointed out, economic division of labour is not the basis of caste. Caste has a mystic and occult foundation. Caste exists even among gods, animals, metres and the seasons. What among men the Brahmin is, that is Agni among the gods, the ram among beasts, the eight syllabic among metres. All these are of the same nature and have sprung from the head of the creator of the world. Similarly the Kshatriya, the Vaisya, and the Sudra have sprung respectively from the arms, the belly and the feet of the creator, their confreres in other spheres of being having the same origin. On this classification rests also the consecration of a Brahmin youth between the years of eight and sixteen, since eight is the sacred member of his caste. For the same reason the period for the Kshatriya boy is between eleven and twenty two, and that of the Vaisya one from twelve to twenty four. For a similar reason the Brahmin kindles his sacrificial fire in spring which is the season for his caste, the Kshatriya in summer, and so forth. The ceremony of shaving the beard is to be performed for a Brahmin youth at the age of sixteen, for one of the Kshatriya caste at the age of twenty two, and for one of the Vaisya caste at the age of twenty four. All these prescriptions have a mystic, magical significance, just like the prescriptions for the seclusion of women during their monthly periods.

The attempt to find an economic basis for the system of castes is as chimerical as the attempt to find a hygienic basis for treating a woman in her monthly periods as a *chandali* on the first day, a *brahmaghatini* on the second, a *rajaki* (washerwoman) on the third, as pure for the husband after a bath in flowing water on the fourth, and for the *devâs* and the *pitris* on the fifth. Menstruation is akin to heat in female animals, and represents the period during which there is a great desire for union with the other sex. But man in his ignorance has given a magical interpretation to what is natural. As Dr. Frazer says, "the object of secluding women at menstruation is to neutralize the dangerous influences, which are supposed to emanate from them at such times. The general effect of these rules is to keep the woman suspended, so to say, between heaven and earth. Being cut off from the earth and the sun, she can poison neither of these great sources of life by her deadly contagion, and she may be considered to be out of the way of doing mischief. The precautions thus taken to isolate or insulate the girl are dictated by regard for her own safety as well as for the safety of others. In short the girl is viewed as charged with a powerful force, which, if not kept within bounds, may prove the destruction both of the girl herself and of all with whom she comes in contact. To repress this force within the limits necessary for the safety of all concerned is the object of the taboo in question." Like the practice of secluding women at the menstrual periods, the practice of shaving the heads of widows has a magical origin. Among all savage and semi-savage races the belief is that the ghosts of the dead hang about places and persons to whom they may be attached; they therefore perform magical rites and ceremonies to drive off the ghosts. The ghost of a dead man is supposed to attach itself to the body of his widow, especially by the hair, as a ghost is supposed to do when it obsesses a woman. Hence the removal of the hair from the head of a widow has come to be regarded as the best means of getting rid of the ghost, in the same way as an Indian magician removes at the last stage a tuft of hair from the head of the obsessed. Suttee also is the result of the belief in a soul. The soul of the dead man was supposed to go with the smoke to the heavenly world. For use in the next life his ornaments, clothing, weapons, and widows were burnt with his body. Widows were therefore forcibly, sometimes stupefied with intoxicants, burnt alive with the dead bodies of their husbands. As an apology for this abomination it was declared at a later stage that "a wife could not bear to survive her husband, but would be prompted by her own faithful, loving, beautiful nature to offer up her life on the pyre which consumed his dead body". We must therefore look for the origins of caste in magic and metaphysics rather than in "an established system of responsible mutual service through division of labour." In a well-organised society all are alike the servants of the same common ideal.

It is a shameless lie to say that at the pinnacle of the caste hierarchy was placed a beggar who renounced and sacrificed things material for things spiritual, when Manu openly declares that the Brahmin is "by right the chief of this whole creation," and that he is entitled to all that exists in the universe by his primogeniture and eminence of birth. The Brahmin was respected, not because "he did not care for wealth, and overcame the fascinations and the temptations of money, and was content to pursue intellectual pursuits and also to devote himself to the spirit and the mind", but because of his birth. The *rishis*, spoken of in the Vedas, were not poor, and if the statements in the Buddhist books may be trusted, many Brahmins at the time of the Buddha must have been wealthy. It is evident from Manu that Brahmins were following different vocations, for he asseverates that, "although Brahmanas employ themselves in all sorts of mean occupation, they must invariably be honoured, for they are something transcendently divine." The Brahmin taught the non-Brahmin the nothingness and the sordidness of the worldly life, and asked him to concern himself with the world of reality, and to resign everything to the "All". Brahmam is the all. Who has a better right to say *aham brahma asmi* than the Brahmin, the representative of the gods on earth, nay, the very god of this earth? Hence everything—property, power, rank, precedence—must be resigned to him. Indeed the Brahmin is a beggar. There are but three ways of living: by working, by begging, or by thieving. Those who do not work, disguise it in whatever fine language, are doing one of the other two. Among the latter must be included the loafers; those who live idly on inherited money; those who live on the surplus work of their fellows; and those who pretend to do brain-work, while they do nothing but repeat hack phrases and glibly utter unintelligible gibberish. The dense ignorance and superstition of the masses of the Hindu society have furnished an opportunity for the breeding of a class of parasites, who have thriven on the life-blood of their victims. It is, however, a consolation that the parasitic habit leads in course of time to the destruction of the parasite itself. Every society needs an organization of some sort. But this organization must be based on solidarity, arising from a sense of community and voluntary co-operation Solidarity implies that each feels answerable for all and all for each. Solidarity in this sense can grow only in an atmosphere of individual freedom. Civilization implies a continually growing freedom and independence of the individual. Every one born must have the same right to live and choose his lot. In so far as one does not encroach on another's liberty, every occupation must be open to one. The grade of one's activity should be determined, not by birth, privilege, power, or volubility, but by his own intellect and will. But this is impossible in a society, in which birth is everything and culture nothing. Culture implies the abolition of classes and castes; the qualities considered superior will not be those immobilized in a special class or caste and protected by special privileges. The standard of one's worth will be his capacity to love.

Caste system is the mainstay of the Hindu religion; it constitutes the common feature of all that passes as Hinduism. "Varnasrama", says Mahatma Ghandhi, "is inherent in human nature, and Hinduism has reduced it to a science. It does attach by birth. A man can not change his Varna by choice." Hinduism is more a religion of usages (*achara*) than of beliefs; it is a religion of a year-long burden of ceremonies. It is a religion for the most part of fear and multitudinous scruples about lawful and unlawful food, inter-dining and inter-marriage. We are told that in the Kali age all other rules, such as those of bathing, prayer (*sandhya*), *tarpana*, have almost disappeared, and the distinction of lawful and unlawful food constitutes the characteristic of the Hindu and distinguishes him from a Mleccha. Revelling in a mythology defying all description and abounding in divinities beyond number, Hinduism reduces in ultimate analysis to the single social fact, the supremacy of the Brahmin. The Brahmin is sacrosanct by birth and eating "pure food". By birth he is qualified to be the depository of truths, otherwise inaccessible to reason. He may follow almost all the professions. He may be an ascetic, a philosopher, a teacher, a writer, a poet, an astrologer, a physician, a beggar, a husbandman, an usurer, an official, a cook a merchant. Yet under all these protean transformations he retains the unique character of being "a god on earth," a deity higher than kings, who must be addressed always lord (*swami, thakur*). The attitude of the Brahmin has been to tolerate the greatest diversity of thought, but to discourage those heresies which lead to the systematic neglect of ancient Brahminical sacraments, or to the disturbance of the position of the Brahmin in the social order. This is the point to which converge all religions, called Hindu, however much they may differ in other respects. Hinduism consists *par excellence* in the superstitions reverence for the Brahmin and the cow. The Brahmin and the cow (*gobrahmana)* constitute in the practical life of the Hindu an inseparable couple. The slaughter of a Brahmin, or a cow, is a sin that can not be expiated; worship of a Brahmin, or a cow, posesses unsurpassable merit.

The system of castes is part and parcel of the Hindu conception of the universe. Speculative activity finds its ultimate expression in the art of social existence. As John Stuart Mill has pointed out, "speculative philosophy, which to the superficial appears a thing so remote from the business of life and the outward interest of men, is in reality the thing on earth, which most influences them, and in the long run overbears every other influence, save those which it must itself obey." By informing the judgment by their truth or warping it by their falsity, speculative opinions consciously, or unconsciously, rule the lives of men. Superstitions, animating the sphere of belief, lead to false principles in the sphere of conduct. Obsessions, swaying the mind, lead it to act out its preconceptions. Like the Muslim and the Christian the Hindu shares with the primitive man the animistic belief in a soul, which has been the source of many a suffering of mankind. The Muslim and the Christian regard each soul as suddenly emerging into existence from nothing, pursuing for a few years its destiny on earth, und falling into oblivion in an apotheosis in heaven, or a damnation in hell. To the Hindu this view appears cruel and unjust. For him the present life is simply a passing phase in an infinite evolution. Mahatma Gandhi tells us that "prohibition against inter-marriage and inter dining is essential for a rapid evolution of the soul." The law of causality, which appears so necessary in the physical world, appears to the Hindu still more necessary in the moral world. Each individual soul is not the result of mere chance, or the caprice of a divine power, but the resultant of an unfathomable past. Each individual soul enjoys in this life the fruit of its own deeds in previous lives. "Those who lead a good life", says the Chandogya Upanishad, "may look forward to being honorably born of a Brahmin mother, a Kshatriya, or a Vaisya; while those who have led a vile life may expect to enter the womb of a bitch, or a sow, or a Chandali." The Brahmin gathers here the fruit of his accumulated merits, while the Chandala expiates his transgressions, though not remembered yet not extinguished, in virtue of a law superior to the immediate exigencies of human reason, a law of retribution infallibly producing its effect somewhere and somewhen not falling within the narrow purview of human vision. This is the Hindu doctrine of Karma, or the transmigration of soul, to which there is no parallel elsewhere. This theory has no relation to the scientific theory of evolution. The biological evolution of mind from the rudimentary psychic life of the primitive cell to the fullness of humanity is entirely foreign to the thought of the Hindu. The passage of the soul through different embodiments in different existences may be a method of purifying itself to return to the Absolute, but this passage is different from what science views as evolution. The goal of the doctrine of Karma is the recovery by the soul of its lost estate, but to science man is the far off event reached by a ceaseless evolution, since life made its first appearance in some early pelagian sea.

The Hindu doctrine of Karma is an adaptation of the primitive belief in reincarnations. Almost all primitive peoples have regarded conception as the reincarnation of a human or animal soul. According to the Brahminic conceptions the soul migrates from man to one or other of the so-called *shadgatis*, just as a man migrates from one house to another, or puts off one coat and dons another according to necessity. It is claimed for this theory that it accounts for the physical, mental, and moral inequalities among men, and enables justice to operate in cases where it has been violated by man, or has failed to operate in the present life. Karma is supposed to be a *natura naturans*, which is capable of rewarding merit and inflicting punishment for wrong. "By Karma or the merit of deeds," says Krishna in the *Bhagavata Purana*, "are living creatures born, by Karma again they enter into dissolution. Pleasure, pain, fear, bliss, all proceed from Karma. If there be a God, the distributor of the fruits of others' actions, he too bestows them on evil doers. There is no such thing as the lord of one that works not. A person receives and gives up various bodies by the instrumentality of Karma, which is itself our friend, our foe, our stranger, our preceptor, our God." This retributive theory supposes that one is punished, because one has sinned in the sight of a power that inflicts punishment. On the other hand, a sane ethics calls that vicious with which the laws of nature connect pain, and thus the viciousness attaches because of the consequential pain rather than the reverse. If occassionally the suffering falls on the evil doer, there is no reason for seeking an explanation in some mysterious nemesis, which is never so successful as any human penal system in saddling punishment on offenders. When the victim is unconscious of his fault, the infliction of punishment can have no moral or disciplinary value. According to modern penology punishment is not avenging wrongdoing, but a means for bettering the wrong-doer and society. Even if we regard rebirths as probationorary, there being no conscious personal identity running through the series of lives, there could be no meaning in speaking of any experience as being carried from one existence to another. If the memory of previous lives be supposed to lie in the subliminal realm, there being no intelligence or moral discrimination in the subconscious, how could there be any mental or moral progress? If after all the happy life of mankind is the greatest good, no distribution either of rewards or punishments is justifiable, except as it helps to realise that good. Whether we enter philosophically into the principles of human conduct, or simply analyse the ideas of right and justice, which have the the common consent of mankind, the infliction of suffering in any case can be right, only when such infliction produces an overbalance of good, irrespective of the innocence or guilt of of the person upon whom it is made. Hence the doctrine of Karma, according to which a man is punished for what is past and irrevocable and for the consideration of that only, must be regarded as one of the crudest conceptions of barbarism. If in one life one has failed to see what is good, what is the guarantee that one would do the same in many?

The doctrine of Karma does not separate the human kingdom from the animal kingdom, and estimate rightly the worth of human personality and the value of individual merit. By ignoring the limits imposed by nature and reason, it assumes that the distinction between the Brahmin and the Pariah is as legitimate and natural as the distinction between man and beast. Nothing can be more fatal to the equal rights of all rational beings than the vague pantheistic connections that are set up by soul theories. It is with a view to explain existing evils that the doctrine of Karma puts an indelible stain on certain men & supports the authority of caste. If pessimism atrophies the instinct of revolt in the heart of man, the fatalism, which is the result of the doctrine of transmigration, extirpates from the mind the idea that existing social conditions may be unjust. By perverting the idea of immortality, the doctrine of metempsychosis perverts at the same time the ideas of merit and demerit, of penalty and recompense, of physical fatality and moral order. Physical evil is considered not only as the necessary consequence, but also as the infallible criterion of moral evil, and the two ideas, not being clearly distinguished, are confounded with each other. The proposition that every demerit entails an affliction passes into the proposition that every affliction involves necessarily a demerit, a sin, and is necessarily a penalty, an expiation. It follows, therefore, that every evil, every suffering, is merited by the person who suffers, though he may not know how or why. When once this monstrosity of an expiation, unaccompanied by the knowledge and memory of the demerit expiated, is regarded as legitimate, the conscience becomes the accomplice of all natutal and social injustices; it accuses none, it protests against none, it revolts against nothing. The heart becomes hardened against the poor, the wretched, and the outcast. Thus has the doctrine of Karma consecrated and eternalised the inequality of conditions, the division of society into castes. Nay more; the deep-rooted prejudices relating to soul and Karma, by raising and preserving barriers against social intercourse between men, tend to create castes. No wonder, therefore, that the religious sects which accepted the doctrine of metempsychosis, although they started with a protest against caste, ultimately succumbed to caste regime. No wonder that those phases of Buddhism, which accomodated themselves to transmigration, could not remove the social evils of India, though they openly revolted against the supercilious claims of the Brahmins.

The doctrine of transmigration of souls stands or falls with the belief in a soul. The belief in souls has originated thus. To struggle for self-preservation is the instinctive impulse of every living being,

This impulse has created in the rational living being, man, a desire for salvation from death. The attainment of this desire is everywhere the problem of religion. In his attempts to find a changeless, deathless life, man has through ignorance fallen a victim to the creations of his own fancy. The horror of death, which is universal among mankind, has, owing to the mystery involved in the decomposition of the dead body and the cessation of relations between the dead person and the survivors, given rise to the obstinate disbelief in the necessity of death. In spite of the invariably disastrous experience of failure, man has incessantly attempted to escape the inevitable doom of death. To satisfy his longing for a deathless life, man has invented immortal souls, which could survive the death of the body. Dream life has led man to regard the dead as really not dead. A little subtle man, or animal, called soul, spirit, or ghost (*atman, pudgala, satkaya, sukshma sarira*) is supposed to dwell inside a man, or an animal, that lives or moves, and to be the active agent in all bodily and mental activities. This soul is supposed to enter the body at conception and quit it permanently at death. It is supposed that one's soul enjoys the fruits of one's actions either by rewards in heaven, or by punishments in hell, or by transmigration into other bodies. Judging, in the light of what he fancies about his own nature, the unknown on which he finds himself hopelessly dependent for the realization of his desires, man has located a soul like his own in every object, almost in every circumstance, which impressed him with a sense of power. The mental condition of the animist or believer in soul is best illustrated by the primitive man, who adores, as a supernatural being endowed with will, the meteoric stone that has fallen rushing from the sky, or by the negro, who thinks a discharging gun to be a living creature. Just as a highly imaginative child symbolizes its fears and peoples darkness with terrifying monsters, so does the man of childish mentality conceive gods and demons. Thus has man peopled the universe with gods and demons, souls like his own but more mighty and capable of doing good or harm. To win their favour and avert their wrath, man has invented prayers, charms, magical formulas, and bloody sacrifices.

The belief in a soul has no basis in modern science. It is the result of a process of abstraction, which the human mind employs in all stages of its development. This operation consists in suppressing, or eliminating, certain aspects of the phenomena under consideration. In the consideration of the complex phenomena constituting a living being, all the physico-chemical phenomena are eliminated, and it is assumed that after the elimination something remains behind. This supposititious mysterious residuum assumes a preponderating importance, and is spoken of as the soul. Since in experience there is a residuum of unexplained facts, it might be difficult to disprove the assumption of a soul, independent of the body, but it is not a scientific hypothesis. It is an outbirth of that sort of reasoning whose guiding principle is: Whatever you are ignorant of is the explanation of what you know. For the animist the body of a living being is merely a statue animated by the soul. With the progress of science animism has retreated to the background Chemical synthesis has produced in the laboratory substances, which were once regarded as the special products of animal or plant activity. Experiment has shown that tissues and even complex organs can under suitable conditions continue to live separate from the body. The phenomena, peculiar to living beings, are due to a physico-chemical state, called the colloidal state. Now this state is not confined wholly to living substance. Many inorganic substances, including some metals, exist in the colloidal form, and in this form they exhibit properties very different from those they possess in other states, but very similar to those of living substance. The colloidal state is a dynamical state of matter and possesses energy, which may be regarded as the probable primary source of energy, appearing in vital phenomena. In their simplest form living beings are small protoplasmic masses, surrounded by an aqueous liquid, in which are suspended other colloids. These small protoplasmic masses are called plastids, or cellules. Some of them have envelopes of inert substances, which are the products of their own activity. In cellules devoid of inert covering there is a continuity of aqueous substance between the living protoplasm and surrounding liquid. Owing to the continuity of the aqueons medium interactions of a colloidal nature continuously take place between the protoplasm and the medium. We can say that the cellule, that is, the continuous protoplasmic mass, is formed from colloidal particles, just as the colloidal particles themselves are formed from the molecules in the solvent. In the case of cellules possessing a membranous envelope, the aqueous continuity between the protoplasm and the medium is brought about through osmosis.

This aqueous continuity is one of the essential conditions of life. In the case of higher animals which live in air, or in water, the body is covered with an impermeable skin, and the exchanges with the medium are confined to particular parts of the organism (intestines, lungs, sensorial surfaces). But in the internal medium confined within the sack formed by the skin, the cellules constituting the animal are in aqueous continuity with the colloids which constitute this medium. No living organism can exist without reactions of equilibrium between the different cellules constituting the organism and the medium, by which the cellules are surrounded. Living beings are transformers of energy, and if all phenomena are due to dyssymetries of energy, there is no reason why those observed in living substance should be excluded.

Life depends upon a supply of food, moisture, and air. Life is a state of the living organism, and can not exist apart from the organism, of which it happens to be the state. When the body of the organism does not exhibit the characteristics of the state, called life, it is said to be dead, or inanimate. In the living body, all the movements are co-ordinated and harmonious; there is continuous adjustment between internal and external conditions, and the various organs of the body exist as parts of a whole. On the other hand in the dead body such movements do not exist; there is no correlation between the various parts of the body; individuality ceases and the parts of the body succumb to the action of external forces. How life originated is not yet known. We have reasons to think that life originated in the primitive oceans when the temperature of their water fell to 45° C. The semination of our globe by means of germs from other celestial bodies is a puerile hypothesis, merely pushing back the problem of the origin of life to mysterious other worlds. The spontaneous generation of a substance, resembling a chemical compound incessantly undergoing destruction, reconstruction, and growth, forming "the physical basis of life", is a more rational hypothesis, though not verified by facts. The study of living bodies has shown that the source of life is in reality an aggregation of three classes of chemical compounds, resembling respectively the white of the egg, fat and sugar. The molecules of the compounds of the first class are formed by the combination of more than a thousand atoms of carbon, hydrogen, nitrogen, oxygen, and sulphur. These are very unstable compounds and undergo decomposition on the feeblest shock, but the products of decomposition are capable of reproducing the original compounds in contact with similar external compounds. All the chemical phenomena of life consist in this destruction and reconstruction of compounds. All phenomena observed in a living being obey the same laws as those outside of it. The possession of the faculties or response by some forms of lifeless matter seems to bridge the gap between the lifeless and the living. These faculties connote the influence of habit and the existence of unconscious recollection. The complex of activities constituting life demands no peculiar type of influence, wholly confined to vital phenomena and absent from all others. Life is nothing more than a combination, made possible by the extreme complexity of protoplasm, of processes each of which taken alone falls within a simpler category, which preceded life in the evolution of the universe. Between inorganic matter and the simplest speck of living protoplasm the gap is being constantly narrowed, and there is only an apparent, not a real, break of continuity. From the protoplasm which can not be said to be either animal. or vegetable, life is seen to be an unbroken chain of gradual ascent. Can we say at what point of this ascent came into existence a soul, distinct from the body and capable of persisting after the dissolution of the physical organism?

While one principle, called the soul, satisfies the animists, the vitalists suppose the existence of two: a thinking soul (*atman*) and a second principle which maintains the vital functions (*prana*). As more and more of these functions are explained by physics and chemistry, the role of the vital principle diminishes. Instead of being the producer of phenomena, it becomes a directing principle, and is attenuated still further to a directing idea Whether this mysterious something, which is supposed to lurk in vital phenomena, be the double of the savage, the soul of the animist, the vital principle of the vitalist, or the the directing principle of some physiologists, it is the product of the same orientation of mind, which consists of two elements, namely: the belief that, when we have eliminated from vital phenomena all observable characteristics, there remains something behind; and the idea that the consciousness of volition corresponds to a reality, which can be explained by an immaterial principle. Neither the endeavours of the innumerable spiritualistic bodies, nor the researches of the Psychical Research Society, have furnished any proof of disembodied souls, or spirits. Owing to the service which the belief in spirits has rendered to mankind as an incentive to overcome the fear of death in battle, as a solace in bereavement, as a stimulant to virtuous life and noble effort, people try to convince themselves of their existence by perverse argument and concocted evidence. What is pleasant and beneficial may be "pragmatically" serviceable, but is not necessarily true. A fundamental *a priori* improbability shrouds all stories relating to spirits. As Edward Clodd puts it, "not on fact, but on sentiment; not on reason but on emotion, do these delusions build their unstable foundations. Impelled by the wish to believe the dupes attend seances by mediums, who like the spirits they pretend to represent, 'love darkness rather than light, because their deeds are evil'. The bias-ruled attitude of the inquirers is wholly uncritical, the power of suggestion paralyses them, they are prepared to see and hear and believe all that they are told, and the unsatiate appetite for the marvellous is satisfied to repletion. All this is emphasised when the sorrowing and the bereaved seek consolation from those, to whom they pay their fees to obtain it."

People come by their beliefs in different ways. Some merely take umbrage in the calm satisfaction of a faith that their belief is the right one and look with pity, contempt, or even horror on all other beliefs. These are like the bird that is said to bury its head in the sand as danger approaches and feel satisfied that there is no danger. More often imposed authority forms the expeditions means of producing a general belief. But this method, though lightly tolerated by the many, is not acceptable to the thoughtful few, who easily penetrate the mist of dogma, and, detecting the pretentiousness of all infallibility, look elsewhere for obtaining a sounder belief. Even when freed from the fetters of authority, men frequently fall victims to their hopes and wishes, and accept views which seem plausible, agreeable, or elevating. Man, it is asserted, is not a mere logical machine, and a place must be conceded to the emotions, the desires, and the will in the determination of belief. If the intellect is unable to affirm or deny definitely, why should not our emotions and desires be permitted to throw themselves in the scale and induce in us "a will to believe"? It is true that the will and the heart control the beliefs and actions of men. To convince is easy when the will to be persuaded is present. It is generally much more efficacious to incite desire than to demonstrate truth.

But a scheme of things satisfying to the heart and the will is more subjective and personal than objective and universal. Unfortunately with the heart and the will man has believed every possible vagary from Rishabha to Gandhi. What is the touchstone with which one may test the creations of desire, the outcome of mere aspiration? From the willingness to believe no progress can result. Only when one scrutinizes one's inclinations and wishes, and cares more for the validity of one's reasoning than for its agreeableness, would it be possible to find the truth. To set store by what is called intuition is to attach significance to all kinds of arrant nonsense and allow words to govern thoughts. As no body can define what intuition is, every body thinks he has it. If knowledge is given in what is spontaneous, every prattling babe is a wise master. Some may consider it a sort of spiritual heroism to believe what is unreasonable. *Credo quia absurdum.* He who questions the validity of reason by means of reasoning deserts his own position. As W. K. Clifford puts it, "belief is desecrated when given to unproved and unquestioned statements for the solace and private pleasure of the believer. . . . Who so would deserve well of his fellows in this matter will guard the purity of his belief with a fanaticism of jealous care, lest at any time it should rest on any unworthy object, and catch a stain which can be never wiped away . . . If belief has been accepted on insufficient evidence, the pleasure is a stolen one. . . . It is simple because it is stolen in defiance of our duty to mankind. That duty is to guard ourselves from such beliefs as from a pestilence which may shortly master our own body and then spread to the rest of the town. . . . It is wrong always, everywhere, and for everyone, to believe anything upon insufficient evidence." The belief in a soul and its immortality has devitalised many men and women, and led them to live an anti-social existence without the enrichment of life.

The hypothesis of a soul may give comfort and satisfaction to some minds, but it renders no service in a scientific psychology. As Prof. James says, "it is not for idle or fantastical reasons that the notion of the substantial soul so freely used by common men and the more popular philosophies, has fallen upon such evil days and has no prestige in the eyes of critical thinkers. It only shares the fate of unrepresentable substances and principles. They are all without exception so barren that to sincere inquirers they appear as little more than names masquerading. You see no deeper into the fact that a hundred sensations get compounded together by thinking that the soul does the compounding than you see into a man's living eighty years by thinking him an octogenarian, or into our having five fingers by calling up pentadactyls. Souls have worn out both themselves and their welcome, that is the plain truth." Normal psychology proves that consciousness can have no existence independent of the organism. Consciousness is known to us only as a phenomenon of life, connected with an organism possessing a nervous system. Consciousness exists for life and not life for consciousness. For, while organic processes continue, consciousness may be lacking, as in perfect dreamless sleep, or in the anæsthetised body, or in a lesion to the brain. Organic processes continue as long as there is life, but consciousness is intermittent and its intermittent character is a premonition of its death. The progress of psychology during the last fifty years has been great, but it has produced nothing to strengthen the popular belief in extra-corporeal spirit agencies. On the other hand, it has made intelligible, conformably to the rest of our knowledge, all such phenomena as have been the props of the ignorant belief in spirits.

Personality is a compound of body and mind, a complex of sensations, ideas, &c. The individualised self is a certain grouping of the elements of experience with the body as its centre, centre of vision, centre of action, centre of interest. Everything circles round the body, and is felt from its point of view. Amidst all changes in consciousness, there is one group comparatively fixed. Our own body is both constant as a group and as a constant item in every field of groups. As Prof. Ward puts it, the body becomes in fact the earliest form of self and serves as the first datum of our later conceptions of permanence and individuality. The unity of what is called personality or individuality consists in the peculiar way in which one's experiences hang together from moment to moment, The conscious rational unity of the "I" is the subjective expression of the physical unity of the whole organism, and does not represent an eternal, transcendental, numerical unity. The word "I" denotes a location, with which are primarily associated certain activities and affectional states. Though the word "I" remains the same, yet its significance continually changes. The sameness is constituted by continuity. The mutual relationship between the varying content of consciousness is determined wholly by that continuity, which is really the work of memory. Every new content of consciousness appears as an object to the personality representing the totality of past experience, which is spoken of as the cognising subject. When memory is diseased, an alteration of personality takes place. Nevertheless, the continuity of the body makes people regard the altered personality as the same individual. The unity of consciousness implies that I am, but does not state that I am a soul, which is eternal, immutable, and permanent. A disembodied personality is, like a square circle, or a barren woman's child, a contradiction in terms.

Though there is no soul, yet death does not end all. Just as the history of each individual does not commence with his birth, so it does not end with his death. The continuity of evolution from the electrón to man is now an almost universally admitted fact. Organic evolution, or the transformation of living beings, both plants and animals, has been established as a scientific fact. Plants and animals are the temporary individualizations of the same life. One germinal substance gathers materials from the outside and develops into the several plants and animals. The individual is only the transient off-shoot of a germ-plasm, having unbroken continuity from generation to generation, from age to age Old individuals originate new individuals, and the old materials are dispersed. In the course of development different species of living beings arise and grow more and more unlike one another They endure for a longer, or shorter, time, and at death suffer dissolution. For science death is destruction, the disappearance of a mechanism, which has only a finite duration. Nature uses up individual lives, just as a fire burns up fuel. "Death is nature's expert contrivance to get plenty of life." Continuity in change is the law of life. Individual death is the penalty that man pays for his high degree of individuation. It is the lives that die but not life. The nature of each man may often be traced through a long series of ancestors and collaterals. This nature passes on through heredity to new bodies. No human being can completely sever himself from other human beings. Man can have neither being not worth in isolation. Human beings form constituent units of society, not only by reason of the inter-dependence of their diverse physical functions, but by reason of their mental inter-dependence. That one is conscious of oneself as a self implies that one can not discriminate oneself except in relation to others. One can not even think oneself as being except as a member of a reciprocal society. Man can not isolate his mental life from that of his fellow-men. He is ever subject to the influence of the community, of which he is a member. He can sever his connection with one circle of men only by joining another. It is indeed exclusively through psychical inter-dependence that human existence as such has been possible. It is through the mutual dependence of their minds upon one another that men are civilized, social, and ethical beings. Each man seems to himself to exist in space, because he measures all distances and directions from his own body. But the corporeal independence of individuals does not establish their psychical separateness. On the other hand, language, art, religion, morality, science prove the psychical inter-dependence of men.

Every man is a component of the general community of human beings. The collective influence is there, and in an immaterial but real way controls the destiny of every man, and every man also contributes his share, however small, to the collective influences, which sway for good or evil the future of mankind. Every man leaves behind him whatever changes he has produced in his surroundings. Even the infant that dies soon after its birth, leaves an impression on its mother. These influences depend on the one hand on the character of the person that has produced them ; on the other hand, their effects and their duration are determined by the persons on whom the influences are exerted. The duration of these influences may be long or short, but they are always present, however much they may become weakened in time. Since men are physically independent of one another, it does not follow that they are also psychically separate from one another. Separateness is due to the overwhelming preponderance of sensory experience, undue attention to individual physical needs, physical sensations, and the centripetal reflexes going from them. But the life of the individual has no meaning apart from the collective life. That which is truly human in each one of us, the true, the beautiful, the good, has something of the universal. Being created and realised only through the communion of minds, it generally breaks through the shackles of individuality, engrafts itself in others and pursues an over-individual life. It is the overcoming of the restrictions of separate ihdividual existence that contributes to the joy of the artist, the social reformer, and all others who co-operate in the welfare of the many and live in the whole. The human race is a vast society, knit together so closely, that, when one part suffers seriously, the other parts also suffer, and when a man errs, the ruin, degradation, and suffering, which his error entails, spread like a miasma round him. What is true of the individual is true of nations. A nation may do everything for itself, not caring for the rest of the world, and bear the consequences of its own limitations.

The negation of the soul naturally leads to the denial of an all-creating *deus extra mundum*, who is simply a replica of the human soul, although endowed with infinite and eternal self conciousness and will. Man simply sees himself, his form, his reason, the best that he has and knows, projected on to the clouds. Theism is a personification of the human mind. "An honest god is the noblest work of man." Neither the method of empiric science, which relies on sensible fact, nor the method of exact science, which relies on mathematical or quasi-mathematical concepts, can justify the belief in God. All arguments for God are the results of the combined suggestions of certain facts, and the moment they affect apodeictic certitude they become unreal. The so-called experiences of the mystics can as little establish the reality of God, as the experiences of those who have drunk themselves into delirium tremens can establish the reality of pink rats. The experiences of the mystics are subjective in character, a feature which inevitably vitiates them. No one can feel sure, not even the mystic himself, that the transcendental or supernatural element in the mystic's experience is not mere subjective illusion. Nor can the mystic demand from others an absolute and unwavering faith in his ecstatic intuition. At best the Hindu yogi, or the Mohammedan fakir, or the Trappist monk, can speak for himself only. The psychology of religious experience proves beyond doubt that the experience varies with the character of the intellectual theory connected with it. A suspicion naturally attaches to a form of experience *(sakshatkara, samyagdarsana)* which can equally establish every view of the supernatural. This inconsistent character of the mystic's knowledge refutes of itself the mystic's claims to immediate insight. The mystic revels in metaphor, and like the poet gives to airy nothing a local habitation and a name. Ecstatic intuition can not establish the truth of a belief, and the placing of intuition above reason would be nothing more than the enshrining and idolizing of unadulterated fatuity.

Facts do not indicate the presence of a purpose in the universe. "To consider the world", as Cardinal Newman says, "in its length and breadth, its various history, the many races of man, their starts, their fortunes, their mutual alienation, their conflicts, and then their ways, their habits, governments, forms of worship; their enterprises, their aimless courses, their random achievements and acquirements, the impotent conclusion of long-standing facts, the tokens so faint and broken of a superintending design, blind evolution of what turn out to be great powers or truths, the progress of things, as if from unreasoning elements, not towards final causes, the greatness and littleness of man, his far-reaching aims, his short duration, the curtain hung over his futurity, the disappointments, the defeat of good, the success of evil, physical pain, mental anguish, the prevalence and intensity of sin, the pervading idolatries, the dreary hopeless irreligion —all this is a vision to dizzy and appal, and inflicts upon the mind a sense of profound mystery, which is absolutely beyond human solution." Facts contradict the notion of order in history and the guidance of man's course by "Divine Providence." There is no similarity between the assumption of Providence and a scientific hypothesis. The end of science has been described as the explanation of the world, the revelation of the real, the unveiling of the causes of nature's processes. No such end is suggested by the actual methods of science. Science is interested only in experience. At the outset experience is but an indefinite multiplicity or a confused mass. The mass of facts is so abundant that no mind can completely grasp and no memory completely retain. Science therefore seeks to colligate these experiences with the object of enabling us to know as much as possible and to communicate our knowledge. To achieve this end it endeavours to find a 'principle' or 'law' that will bind all facts harmoniously together. Hence science can advance only by trying hypothesis after hypothesis, until it reaches one that comprehends all the facts. This has always been the method of science. The practical end of science is served equally well, whether its hypotheses correspond to reality or not. It is not necessary that a scientific hypothesis be true or even probable; the one thing required of it is to reconcile calculation and observation. It may involve unintelligible elements, self-contradictions, phantoms of the imagination, but all this is a matter of indifference, if calculation and observation tally, as, for example, the hypothesis of relativity of Einstein. The man of science feels no pang in dropping his hypothesis; for him the facts of experience are everything. Once he found no prospect of attaining his end without postulating the existence of an æther, an all-pervading medium, which can behave both like a very elastic solid and an extremely tenuous gas, but Einstein finds no use for this subtle substance. To say that anything was effected by God is not a scientific hypothesis. A scientific hypothesis gives us a classification of laws, and points to new experimental methods, thereby enabling us to include a multitude of facts and details in a simple mathematical expression. Does the postulation of God or Providence do anything similar? On the other hand, it only indicates our innate dislike to a confession of ignorance. A scientific hypothesis has not the kind of validity that belongs to a scientific law; the latter does not run the risk of being replaced by another law. A scientific law is not a reality in itself, but a formula invented by the human mind as a substitute for things to render them comprehensible, to represent them in accordance with the laws of thought. A scientific law does not claim any validity other than empirical verifiability. All verification consists in comparing forecasts with experience, and the more uniform the correspondence between the two the more complete is the verification, and the greater the confidence inspired by the law. It is a principle of logic that from objects of experience other objects of experience may be inferred, but not existences that could not be experienced at all. Can any empirical verification be provided for God? God belongs to the realm of the Absolute, with which science does not coquet. Science is confined wholly to the realm of relativity and contingence. Science accepts only that as *real* which can be tested by the criterion of universal experience. Science does not pretend to find solutions for enigmas born of a mystic mentality. That is why the Sastras, which are the only guide to the Brahmam surpassing all reasoning, tell us that "God is not known by inference, but only by those on whom he bestows his grace, even a particle of it." That is why the Supreme Being Vishnu is pleased only by the worship of those that do the duties prescribed by their castes. That is why, when reason is suppressed and *bhakti* is attained, the *jiva* "is joined unto Brahmam as one spirit enjoying

His bliss for ever."

To err is a characteristic of the imperfect man; to do nothing would be immaculate conduct. To attribute this imperfection to original sin is hideous. Man is not evil by nature. No external master has taught man his moral duties, his rules of life. The experience of life has revealed them to him, has rather imposed them on his will than made them known to his intellect. This truth must be obvious even to those who believe in a revelation. For, no such revelation would be understood, if the mind of man were a complete stranger to the ideas put forward by the revelation, and it would be specially powerless to impose on man a rule of life entirely unrelated to the needs of his life, or to attract him towards an ideal which is not in harmony with aspirations already working in him. If the individual does have external masters, they can be only human beings, for the human race can apprehend nothing except through itself and its own experience in the moral sphere as in the domain of science. But this morality, which has originated spontaneously in relation to the conditions of existence and social life in particular, is not so much a product of intelligence, of reflection, as the result of an instinctive adaptation. When man begins to examine himself and reflect on what has been achieved by him, he finds this spontaneous morality already present in him in the form of a conscience. He further finds it outwardly sanctified by the rules and traditions of a social order which he can not eschew. Though often treated as an absolute and infallible judge of right and wrong, this conscience is only the complex result of human progress and civilization. Far from being a great educator, it is itself the product of many influences. A child, could it grow up alone in a wilderness, would be wholly devoid of a conscience. Domesticated animals such as dogs and horses, knowing precisely what is expected of them, exhibit unquestionable traces of a conscience, which is the result of the training to which they have been subjected. The principal and precise purpose of all discipline and training is to create, by the formation and development of a conscience, a perfect accord between one's ethical ideal and actual life. Variable according to the stage of culture of mankind, at a given moment one's conscience is truly the inspirer of one's conduct, provided that it has already been formed. The discord between one's actual life and one's ideal as represented by his conscience is the feeling of sinfulness. It is a vulgar idea that the right is a settled something to which every one has to adjust his opinions and actions. History and anthropology show that it is capable of any expansion, proclaiming its own prerogative to exist, even by making a stand against the whole world. The perfect accord between ethical knowledge and will is the subjective criterion of all moral life, while the advancement of mankind forms the objective test.

Every system of morality is a body of imperfect social generalizations, expressed in emotional terms. To get at its truth it is useful to omit the emotion and ask ourselves what those generalizations are. We then find that moral ideas have nothing to do with the belief in supernatural beings or with the faith in a future life. It is ridiculous to say that man avoids vice and practises virtue, is truthful, merciful, loving and kind for fear of an invisible police. Supernatural beings being only creations of human fancy, they can be endowed only with such qualities as man already possesses. The moral character of supernatural beings can not but vary with the ethical standards of their worshippers. Men have attributed to their gods everything that is a shame and reproach among men—theft, adultery, and mutual deception. As man advances to higher stages of morality, his earlier conceptions of gods no longer satisfy him, and they are reconstructed to meet his new ideals. The history of religious thought proves this beyond doubt. Nor is the belief in immortality helpful to the moral life. As already shown, there is no evidence for the existence of a soul and its post-mortem psychic activity. Setting the question of the existence of the soul aside, history shows that the greatest iniquities are possible in conjunction with the fear of hell. History further shows that too much thought about the future life has destroyed enthusiasm for the enrichment of the present life. He who believes that the immortality of the individual soul secures for his conscious self an eternity of existence, and that this earthly life is merely a brief prelude thereto, having no other value than being a period of test for the future life, will prefer a cloistered life of prayer or pious meditation to a strenuous endeavour to live the largest and fullest life, which will help the onward progress of mankind. The horror at the thought of personal extinction is the natural expression of the deeply-rooted physical will to live so characteristic of every living being. Belief in personal immortality is merely an illusion born of the natural instinct for the preservation of life. But illusions, threats, hypothetical promises can not be of much avail in the development of a moral personality. Only by facing facts will man gain strength to live a full and worthy life without need of a reward in a future life.

It is of the essence of moral duty that it should be imposed by the nature of man, which sets before him the ideal of a perfect life. The actual needs of man and the realities of life are enough to foster a moral nature. Man desires always to get rid of suffering and sorrow and enjoy bliss. Man's nature is such that he can not live in a state of isolation. Man has always been a gregarious being. Only by sharing the society of his fellows the animal man has become a human being. The social impulse belongs to the very fundamental impulses of man. The social impulse leads to reciprocal activity, to mutual influence, to mutual giving and receiving, to mutual suffering and enjoying. No man can realise all his desires without the help of others. It is by life in common that man has been able to achieve that wonderful work, called science, whose applications are so indispensable to individual life. Science is the means by which he gets rid of his sufferings and sorrows. The perfection of science is the common aim of all mankind. But this can be achieved only in a moral atmosphere, which suppresses the lower elements in man and prevents the prostitution of science to his own destruction. "Science is neither the up-builder nor the destroyer. It is the docile slave of its human masters. It will appear as the one or the other, according as the moral outlook of the latter is derived from a progressive and deepening sense of responsibility, awakened by the realization of the true position, which man occupies with regard to the external realities of nature, or an impossible compromise between this and the old mystic mythologies." Without morality happiness is impossible. If happiness is the end of each individual, one can not attain it except by striving to make others happy, by raising them to that ideal of humanity which he has found for himself. The highest aim of society is the happiness of all its members by the creation in them of a feeling of oneness and not of disparateness as caste does.

The baser emotions, such as anger, hatred, fear, jealousy, spring from the need of food and the individual interests connected with reproduction. Attention to these tends to perpetuate the restrictions of self or separate individual existence.

On the other hand all human virtues, which draw the attention away from the restrictions of self, tend towards expansion. Broadly speaking the highest morality consists in doing everything for some one else in preference to one's self. The superior man is not the man, whose sole and exclusive aim is his ego and its welfare, nor the man of power, nor the self-seeker of domineering will, but the man with a broad comprehensive mind and a great compassionate heart. Justice is often described as the greatest gift of man. Nothing can be farther from the truth than this. Justice is a disrupting quality, while man has progressed by union and self-sacrifice. An eye for an eye, a tooth for a tooth, blood for blood, measure for measure: this is what justice demands. *Summum jus, summa injuria.* Justice demands punishment for wrong, and respect and protection for the rights of others as well as one's own by lawful means. Justice requires us to do unto others, as we wish they should do unto us. The bandage over the eyes of the representation of justice symbolises its mechanical character. That justice is not final is proved by every sovereign power reserving to itself the right of pardon. True progress needs some sacrifice on the part of those who benefit by mere justice. While justice is concerned with man as he is at present, magnanimity directs its eye to the future man. Magnanimity requires us to resign claims to which we are legally entitled, so that the advancement of our interests may not cause relatively greater damage to those of others. The question of justice never enters into the discussion of human affairs, except where the pressure of necessity is equal; the powerful exact what they can, and the weak grant what they must. The joy of magnanimity consists in giving more than one can receive. Nature is full of disharmonies, and society is the anonymous author of many existing miseries, so that it is but right that society should repair the consequences of its imperfections and its past iniquities. Not only are the murderer, the thief, the lier, the adulterer, and the drunkard responsible to society, but society is equally responsible for breeding such characters. A perfect social system would apportion everybody's advantages and burdens exactly according to what he needed for the function suitable to him. The magnanious man makes himself the voluntary instrument of this 'social justice' by accepting some personal self-sacrifice for removing evils for which he is not personally responsible. It s the highest aim of moral training to call forth that energetic manliness and stern nobility, which requires no compensation in the way of reward, either in heaven or on earth but finds its highest enjoyment in the consciousness of progress.

Some attempt the worship of self-regarding passions on the ground of evolution. To these the course of evolution is a struggle, and those that fight most successfully and survive in the struggle are the fittest. This view of evolution has gained plausibility from the fact that the uncivilized races have often been exterminated by the civilized. But it does not ask why we prefer the exterminators to the exterminated. It is not because of the fulfilment of any law of evolution, but because the exterminators possess all those goods, which are summed up in the word civilization. Now civilization implies the avoidance of waste of energy and the economising of labour. This is no other than the mastery of the forces of nature so as to make them serve man's instinctive cravings. This has been achieved by the freest co-operation. Man, though nearly always engaged in a desperate struggle with his environment and often fighting with his fellows, is a social being, who has long since learned that co-operation and organization are as essential to human welfare, as are struggle, rivalry, and competition. Ever since his first appearance man has never lived in isolation, but in groups, such as families, hordes, clans, village communities, cities, states, nations, confederacies, etc., within which the practice of mutual aid or co operation, has largely supplanted, or at least modified, the habit of struggle or rivalry. Civilization is therefore not the result of ferocity, struggle and competition but of mutual aid and utility. If civilizations have fallen and perished, they have done so through slavery, serfdom, greed, rivalry, conquest, immorality and idleness. The decay and death of civilizations have everywhere been the result of the combination of the dominant ruling families and their subsequent struggles for power. It is indeed true that the struggle for existence has played a part in the intellectual and ethical development of man. But this very development has made him see that the mere struggle for existence is a hindrance to the evolution of his intelligence and might over nature. Political history confirms this. All political history is nothing more than the effort of an increasing number of individuals, who, seeing advantages in organization endeavour to modify the social structure so that these benefits may be increased, not only for a ruler or a privileged class, but for all participating in the organization. I struggle is the condition of progress in the living world, there can be none without mutuality and the co-ordination of forces.

The denial of soul and God does not imply the denial of all religion. Religion is born of the feeling of dependence on unknown factors in man's endeavour towards self-preservation, and includes all attempts to get over that feeling of dependence. In the shaping of these attempts imagination, emotion, and ignorance have played a dominant part, and the results are magic, sacrifices, and superstition. One such attempt is the invention of some unseen higher power or powers that can help man in shaping his destiny. To the primitive mind this power is a being to be prayed to for material help. At a later stage of culture when man feels his moral failure, this being becomes a means of escaping from sins and entering on a better course of life. At a still higher stage this power becomes a contrivance for securing the observance of moral rules. Having invoked God to save him from his troubles and trammels, man finds himself in the clutches of a new tyrant with whom he has to make terms. God has become the great mystery, awfully weighing on the mind of man. But the essence of religion is not God, but a larger, more satisfying life. Life, more life, is the end of life. Religion is essentially a plan of action to realize man's hope of a life free from suffering and sorrow. Even in Christian countries the leaders of thought and some of the rank and file overtly disavow their acceptance of the traditional belief in a divine father, who directly communicates with man. Slavery, feudalism, theocracy, autocracy are always associated with theism. Theism has become logically impossible. Theological efforts at reconstruction of theism under the guise of immanence are a proof of the failure of theism and the necessity to keep in check pantheistic intrusions. Pantheism is vigorously pushing its way in modern religious life in the form of Vedanta, Theosophy, Christian Science, New Thought, and so forth. Mysticism seems to exert a fascinating and soporific influence on certain minds. Pantheism views the vilest actions as well as the worst passions as the manifeststions of the one Absolute Being, the Great All, or the Infinite Life. Of this Absolute Being nothing can be said except that "it is not this, not that." All substantial monisms land us in "nothing", which passes into "being" through "becoming". Pantheism makes man a puppet and God the puppet master (*sutradhar*). By utter disregard of speculative consistency and the most flagrant contradictions some forms of pantheism attempt to escape its immoral consequences. Between pantheism and materialism there is no essential difference; matter or æther, possessing the potency of life and thought, does not differ in essence from the pantheistic Brahmam. Pantheism and materialism are but different aspects, and the passage from the one to the other is easy, and takes place according as the poetical or practical sentiment is predominant. Hegelian pantheism passed easily into Feuerbach's materialism. The Great All of Pantheism has passed in Positivism into the *Grand Etre*, a poetical personification of humanity as a growing, self-perfecting organism of moral units. Positivism revolts against God-worship, but substitutes in its place man-worship. The latter is as vapid as the former. Man, as he is, swayed by sensuality, unreason, strange stupidities, mighty passions, devastating fears and hates, may call forth pity but not worship. A philosophy of some sort is necessary to every individual. An intelligent evaluation of circumstances and the adoption of a deliberate attitude towards them is absolutely necessary for every man. Every one is aiming at salvation and mental peace. Hence there is no phase of culture without religion in its right sense. Humanity is a part of the blind energy immanent in the universe. By virtue of this energy manifested in his will and intelligence, man is progressing onward by the indomitable promptings of his own nature The human will is a will to live, to remove obstacles, to solve riddles, to extend horizons, to enrich this life. The ideal of asceticism represents human effort as essentially a sacrifice of one part of man's nature to another to live in the latter more completely, but the ideal of culture is a perfectly developed personality, which can be evolved only by the harmonious development of all parts of human nature in just proportion. True emancipation can come only by abandoning the struggle for private happiness and devoting oneself to a larger life and wider interests. What is wanted is not worship but service in the evolution of a superior humanity, which shall be guided by reason, vivacity of intelligence, grace of culture, high and disinterested motives of action, and generous enthusiasm. "Religion does not brood over a future life, but is intensely occupied with the present; it does not surmise something behind nature, but contemplates nature itself; it does not shrink from political organization, but is itself the soul of all healthy political organization; it does not damp enjoyment, but is itself the principle of all rich enjoyment; it is not self-conscious or self-absorbed, and does not make us anxious about our own fate, but is the principle which destroys self and gives us strength to rise above personal anxieties."

All progress in religion consists in a reconciliation between religion and science. Is any such reconciliation possible between science and Brahminism, or Hinduism, as it is usually called? Hinduism adopts and adapts foreign ideas, so long as they are not antagonistic to the system of castes, the revelatory character of the Vedas. and the belief in a soul. The caste system is the chief strength and the basic principle (*mula mantra*) of Hinduism. Caste is a necessary adjunct to one born as a Hindu, which can not be helped whether it be advantageous or inconvenient. By renouncing caste a Hindu becomes a Mlecchа. As the Brahmin author of the *Hindu Dharma Tatva* says, "it is by means of caste distinctions that in the Bharatakhanda the Hindu religion has been so well preserved. These caste distinctions are the chief support of the Hindu religion; when they give way, there can be no doubt that the Hindu religion will sink to destruction." Hinduism is a religion of *achara* and not dependent on the beliefs one holds. These usages and ceremonies rest on the authority of *sruti* and *smriti*, that is on the Vedas and the Sastras. *Achara* is the chief basis of modern Hindu society, and *achara* is the deliberate disavowal of the liberty of thought and action. Says Krishna to Arjuna in the *Gita*: "He who abandons the dictates of the Sastras and acts according to his own sweet will, does not get the right fruits of his action, attaineth neither happiness nor the highest good. Wherefore, Arjuna thy authority is Sastra in determining what is fit and unfit to be done, thou shouldst perform those works which are declared by the commandments of the Sastras." One may know a certain thing to be black, but one must regard it as white, if *sruti* says so. The Hindu regards the bone and ordure of animals as unlean, but he takes conch-shells and cow-dung as pure, because *sruti* says so. Birth confers on the Brahmin the prerogative of interpreting the Sastras, and he claims to be the depository of truths inaccesible to reason. Ecclesiaticism prevents reason from making claims to the preserve of revelation, and endeavours to lay reason to sleep. Experience and reason are the only instruments of science. Hinduism regards the Veda as a revelation, which one must follow like "one who, without possessing the sense of sight himself, has to depend upon that of another." The attitude of Brahminism towards the teachings of science is clearly illustrated by the position taken by the orthodox astronomer Brahmagupta in relation to the right explanation of solar and lunar eclipses. In the first chapter of his *Brahmasiddhanta*, he writes: "Some people think that the eclipse is not caused by the Head (Rahu). This, however, is a foolish idea; for he is in fact who eclipses, and the generality of inhabitants of the world say that it is the Head who eclipses. The Veda, which is the word of God from the mouth of Brahma, says that the Head eclipses, likewise the book *Smriti*, composed by Manu, and the *Samhita*, composed by Garga, the son of Brahma. On the contrary, Varahimihira, Srisena, Aryabhata, Vishnuchandra maintain that the eclipse is not caused by the Head, but by the moon and the shadow of the earth, in direct opposition to, and from enmity against, the just mentioned dogma. For, if the Head does not cause the eclipse, all the usages of the Brahmins, which they follow at the time of an eclipse, such as rubbing themselves with warm oil and bathing and then performing certain prescribed rites, would be illusory and not e rewarded by heavenly bliss. If a man declares these things to be illusory, he stands outside the generally acknowledged dogma, which is not permitted. Manu says: 'When the Head (Rahu) keeps the sun or moon in eclipse, all waters on earth become pure, and in purity like the water of the Ganges." The Veda says: "The Head is a son of a woman of the Daityas, called Sainaka." Hence people practise the well-known works of piety, and therefore those authors must cease to oppose the generality for everything, which is in the Veda, Smriti, and Samhita, is true." Can the Brahmin bid farewell to his cherished beliefs and practices, such as *upanayana*, *gotra*, *pravara*, *agnihotra*, *saptapadi*, *sandhya*, *tarpanà*, *sraddhà* and so forth and still retain his Brahminism? The scientific attitude of mind refuses to have regard for our hopes and fears, loves and hates, desires, tastes and interests, in short, our whole subjective emotional life, in understanding the world. Any reconciliation between Brahminism and science could be effected only by an ingenious and methodical cheating, which would only degrade the people who tolerated it. We can not gather grapes of thorns, nor pluck figs out of thistles. Till the teachings of science take the place of speculative opinions, social progress can be neither certain nor swift. Science is the great instrument of social change, all the greater because its object is not change but knowledge. What is injurious to the intellect can not be beneficial to the moral life. He, who loses confidence in intellectual certitude, loses at the same time his confidence in moral certitude. If the standard is not truth but the expedient and the reputable, sincerity must yield place to hypocrisy. No wonder that hypocrisy has made men's minds the fanes of many an outworn worship. The true view of the universe alone can give man freedom.

Progress comprises all those healthy. beneficial tendencies and movements that make for a better society. It is force of habit that makes people blind to waste and tyranny. The *Weltgeschicte* has many paths. Revolution is as much a path of progress as evolution. The universal urge for progress may manifest itself in either way. Revolution may confer blessings which evolution may take a long time to give. "When the country is deluged with flood and there is no fixed course for a boat to take, it goes faster to its destination by following an undefined course than it would do by taking the zig zag course of a well-defined river in the dry season." History shows that only revolutions have given the masses the chances of cultural progress. Nothing is gained by bemoaning the loss of historic continuity. Historic continuity may represent either progress or regress. Appeals to past glory, picturesque historicity. and so-called civilization may tickle people's vanity, but will serve only to hinder onward progress. Every step of progress involves the repudiation of old institutions and obligations. A clean sweep and forgetting of the past may sometimes be as beneficial as remembrance of the past and taking pride therein. Conformity to dead views and usages can only scatter one's force and blur one's character. Those that aim at progress can not help cutting themselves adrift from such doctrines and institutions as stand in the way of progress. The two pillars of the old class system of Germany were the reserve officer and the official with academic training. A line of demarcation completely separated the world of these from the world below, which nobody overstepped. The democratic revolution did away with these. To attain national unity the Japanese discarded their caste system, and removed all sources of social cleavage. The *Samurai*, who were at one end of the ladder, gave up their long standing privivileges, and the disabilities of the *Eta*, who, like the Pariahs, were looked upon as defiled, were removed. Progress implies individual freedom and liberty, and these establish the right of every one to seek one's mate where one will. Without some intermixture of blood there emerges no feeling of solidarity. A civilized government ought to enact such laws as shall afford the freest social opportunity without barriers of colour, class, or race Unfortunately governments have a tendency to ally themselves with ecclesiasticism, as it is advantageous to them to prevent people from thinking about the foundations of society. We are told that the caste system is the outcome of a tolerance of racial differences. A tolerance of racial differences can be achieved only by the willingness to treat all human beings as participating in a common human destiny. The aim of progress is solidarity. On the other hand, caste breeds repulsion and opposition. The division between caste and caste is so sharp that only by the aid of adventitious interests, interests determined by tradition and religion, is community maintained. A fictitious unity is maintained at the expense of the intrinsic interests of the community. Progress is possible only by the transformation of like interests into common interests, and the exclusiveness of caste bars the way. The divisions of caste would destroy community, were it not that extrinsic common interests, traditional and religious, prove substitutes for those intrinsic common interests, which caste system rejects. As F. H. Giddings points out, the original and elementary fact in society is the consciousness of kind. It is about the consciousness of kind, as a determining principle, that all other motives organize themselves in the evolution of social choice, social volition, or social policy. Our conduct towards those whom we feel to be most like ourselves, is instinctively and rationally different from our conduct towards others, whom we believe to be less like ourselves. The spirit of caste stands in the way of the spontaneous recognition of fellowship, a consciousness of kind.

The spirit of nationality is no better than the spirit of caste. Nationality has sentiment, pride, and fanaticism for its basis, and is found on analysis to be no more than imaginary justification of the will to power and possession. Nationalism is ths camouflage by which hooliganism masks its true nature. Intense nationalism tends to blind fanaticism and destroys the consciousness of brotherhood of man towards man. A world made up of separate nations means a world of states with separte interests, which bring about rivalry and militarism. If one must learn to subordinate one's own good to that of others, there can be no valid ground for stopping short of the whole human race. All talk of diversity in the destiny of nations is mere cant. The real problem for all nations is the preparation of men for noble ends. "Truth is the same for all nations, but each nation has its own lies, which it speaks of as its idealism." Science and trade are practically proving that mankind is one great commonwealth. Only the impersonal cosmic outlook of science will bring about real emancipation. A noble humanity can be produced only through personal individual development, the increase of knowledge, and the sense of responsibility enabling men to act in accordance therewith. They speak of the reconstitution of our life, economic, social and educational, on the basis of a spiritual communism. We know not what this spiritual communism may be, but we know that science is an actual and practical communism. Common ownership of all its acquisitions is the very breath of its life. Individualism or nationalism of any kind is antagonistic to the fertility and growth of science. Resting on the blind belief in soul, its Karma, and its transmigration, caste can never bring about that social development which is the necessary condition for the growth of science. Caste makes it impossible to understand and estimate the claims of others in comparison with our own and to enter into relations with an ever-widening community. Hindu spiritually is the index of an early stage of conscious life, which is lacking in all those qualities which make for social development. The inevitable result of Hindu spirituality is the galling yoke of inferiority trampling a large portion of mankind. Only by discarding caste and all doctrines that give it succour will such mingling be possible as will create good fellowship and complete equality. Progress consists not in the trappings of glittering mechanism, nor in high buildings and long streets, but in the breaking down of barriers, in the release of individuality, in the enrichment of personality, in the widening of community. The ideal of progress is the completest possible harmony of all men, all interests, and all communities.

The belief in a soul, surviving the death of the body

and living an eternity of existence, is in perfect discord with the scientific conception of the universe. No rational mind can be duped by the savage theory of the transmigration of souls masquerading under the flowing drapery of retributive justice. The doctrine that man's certain life here and now is but a prelude to a hypothetical future existence has led men to look upon actual human life as a means and not as an end in itself. It has minimised the dignity and importance of the present life in comparison with life in a world beyond, and thus led men to believe that it is a matter of spiritual indifference whether the earthly life, forming a short stretch of road leading to heaven, is rough and stony, dark and narrow, or broad, bright with sunshine, and carpeted with flowers. No wonder that this religious doctrine, consciously and logically developed, has led to a social hierarchy, which ignores the claims of the majority of men to live a large and true life. In this wrong ideal lies the root of our backwardness in bringing the knowledge we possess to bear upon our conduct. In the false antithesis between the material and the spiritual is the fundamental error which is doing incalculable mischief to mankind, immeasurably retarding human progress. When men shall recognise the unity of all that is, the inter-relation and inter-dependence of the material and the psychical, they will make mighty strides in the advancement of human welfare. In proportion as man recognises that the fundamental principles in accordance with which his own nature develops, which his own mental processes reflect, regulate also the transformations of the whole universe, organic and inorganic, in that measure does his intellectual horizon expand. Just as the recognition of our community of nature with that which is external to and beyond our individual selves increases our wisdom, so does the recognition of the corresponding community of interest develop our morality. The more perfectly we come to recognise that of which we are a part is not merely a household, a family, a class, a district, or a country, but all mankind, not to speak of the whole universe, the more successful shall we be in living, beautiful, happy lives.